1.b

Jon Hird with Jonathan [illegible]s

Inside Out

Grammar Companion

Advanced

MACMILLAN

Macmillan Education
Between Towns Road, Oxford OX4 3PP, UK
A division of Macmillan Publishers Limited
Companies and representatives throughout the world

ISBN-10: 1-4050-8210-0
ISBN-13: 978-1-4050-8210-5

Text written by Jon Hird with Jonathan Marks

First published 2006

Page layout by Anthony Godber
Illustrated by Kathy Baxendale, Mark Draisey and Bill Piggins
Cover design by Andrew Oliver

The publishers would like to thank Gill Francis, the editor, for all her hard work.

The authors and publishers are grateful for permission to reprint the following:
Extract from 'That's the way the ball bounces', first published in *Associated Press* 14.04.05, reprinted by permission of Reprint Management Services.

Printed and bound in Spain by Edelvives

2010 2009 2008 2007 2006
10 9 8 7 6 5 4 3 2 1

Contents

1 Identity (1)

Adverbials

Adverbials comprise:

Adverbs: *always, actually, basically, hopefully, happily, badly, only, almost, really, completely, primarily, extremely*

Adverb phrases: *very beautifully, rather well, very much, quite easily, extremely carefully, quite perfectly, dreadfully badly*

Prepositional phrases: *at the moment, to some extent, on the whole, at eight o'clock, with a smile, by accident, in Paris*

Noun phrases: *every day, last Friday, the day before yesterday, a great deal, the next night, a long time ago*

Adverbials fulfil a number of functions. You can use them to add information about a verb by:

- saying **where** something happens — Do you live **round here**?
- saying **when** something happens — They moved out of the city **ages ago**.
- saying **how long** an action continued for — He's been dreaming about it **for months**.
- saying **how often** or **frequently** something happens — We used to visit my grandparents **most Sundays**.
- saying **how** something happens — She sang **beautifully**.
- indicating the **degree** or intensity of a state or action, or **emphasizing** it — I like my job **immensely**. I **thoroughly** enjoy long walks in the country at weekends.
- indicating **how probable** something is — I **probably** won't be able to see you this afternoon.

You can use them to add information about an adjective, for example by grading it. Some grading adverbs are *awfully, dreadfully, exceptionally, extremely, fairly, greatly, highly, horribly, hugely, incredibly, moderately, phenomenally, really, remarkably, terribly* and *very*.

He was **extremely** happy to see her. It was **fairly** hot for the time of year.

You can also use them to add information about a participle, for example *widely (appreciated), much (loved), largely (forgotten)* and *hopelessly (lost)*.

She is **highly** respected in her field. He was **much** loved by all who knew him.

You can use them to comment on a clause or sentence, or to focus attention on one part of it.

Generally speaking, the trains are very efficient.
I've **actually** lived here for five years now.
Frankly, I didn't believe a word they said.
Fortunately he was accepted into medical school.

Position of adverbials

There are three possible positions for adverbials in a sentence.

Initial position You can put most types of adverbial at the beginning of the sentence, for example in accounts of events, or for emphasis. This applies especially to adverbials consisting of prepositional phrases.

In 2005 he finally retired from his job. **On the whole** I prefer to eat organic food.

Mid position You tend to put one-word adverbials of frequency, probability and emphasis in the mid-position.

- between the subject and the main verb — I **often** forget to lock the back door at night.
- after the verb *be* (especially adverbs of frequency) — He was **always** the last to arrive.
- between an auxiliary and the main verb — We'll **probably** come and visit you sometime in May.
- either before or after a negative auxiliary — They **probably** didn't mean to offend you.

Final position You tend to put longer adverbial phrases and adverbials of manner (how something happens) into the final position.

The orchestra played **with more enthusiasm than skill**.

Note: Changing the position of the adverbial sometimes changes the meaning of the sentence.

Only Sarah has Pierre's e-mail address. (= no-one else has it)

Sarah **only** has Pierre's e-mail address. (= and nothing else)

1 (1) Practice

1 Which of the underlined adverbials in the biography add information about:

a) where something happens in Kentucky

b) when something happens in 1963

c) a participle

d) an adjective

@ http://www.starsearch/biographies/johnnydepp.html

JOHNNY DEPP

John Christopher Depp II, widely known as Johnny Depp, was born in Kentucky in 1963 into a family of mostly British, German and Cherokee descent. Aged seven, his family moved to Florida and he grew up there. His mother bought him a guitar around the age of 13 and Depp soon began playing in local bands. At 16, he suddenly decided to drop out of school to become a rock musician. His band, aptly named *The Kids*, was modestly successful, but they split up when he married the drummer's sister. Depp then turned to acting. He appeared in his first film, *A Nightmare on Elm Street*, in 1984 and his first lead-role was in the hugely successful *Edward Scissorhands* six years later. Since then, he has appeared in a diverse range of Hollywood blockbusters, including *What's Eating Gilbert Grape*, *Charlie and the Chocolate Factory* and, more recently, as Jack Sparrow in the *Pirates of the Caribbean* series. He lives with his family in Los Angeles and the South of France.

page: 1|2|3|4|5|6|7|8|9 Next page

2 Rewrite the sentences about actress Keira Knightly with the adverbials in *italics* in a natural position. Use the adverbials in the order they are given.

a) She was born *in London; on March 26th 1985*
She was born in London on March 26th 1985.

b) Her father was a successful actor and her mother a playwright, so she has been exposed to the acting profession. *moderately; continually; all her life*

c) She started acting and made her film debut. *at an early age; in 1994*

d) Her breakthrough role was in the popular *Bend it Like Beckham*, which was released. *phenomenally; in 2002*

e) The filming was demanding because of the rigorous football training she had to do. *very; physically; extremely; virtually; every day*

f) The success of the film opened the door for her. *quickly; into Hollywood*

g) Her role in the successful *Pirates of the Caribbean* blockbusters has cemented her up-and-coming position. *hugely; firmly; in international cinema*

h) Besides acting, she models and was voted the world's sexiest movie star. *currently; recently*

3 Match the sentences with the sentence 1 or 2 that has similar meaning.

a) Only Pete and Sam went for a drink. 2
b) Pete and Sam only went for a drink. 1
1) Pete and Sam went for a drink and did nothing else.
2) Pete and Sam went for a drink on their own.

c) Just Dina called me. ☐
d) Dina just called me. ☐
1) Nobody called me except Dina.
2) Dina called me a few minutes ago.

e) I particularly don't like Bar Soleil. ☐
f) I don't particularly like Bar Soleil. ☐
1) Bar Soleil is okay, but not my first choice.
2) Bar Soleil is awful.

g) The party isn't definitely cancelled. ☐
h) The party definitely isn't cancelled. ☐
1) The party may go ahead.
2) The party is going ahead.

1 *Identity (2)*

Phrasal verbs with objects

You can combine a verb and a particle to extend the usual meaning of a verb or to create a new meaning, different from any that the verb has on its own. There are three basic types of phrasal verb that take an object.

Type 1: not separable

verb + particle + object

I **came across** an interesting article in this magazine.

I haven't read it properly; I**'ve** only **looked through** it.

I'm going out. Can you **look after** the children for an hour or so?

I don't want to **go against** the wishes of my parents.

They met at a party and **fell for** each other immediately.

Type 2: separable

There are two possible ways of ordering the phrasal verb and the object. Most phrasal verbs can have either order.

1. verb + object + particle

They spent a fortune **doing** that old house **up**.

He**'ll be bringing** the issue **up** at the next meeting.

I**'m putting** the call **through** to his office now.

I went to the station to **see** my mother **off**.

2. verb + particle + object

We **brought up** the subject of Harry's birthday party.

John and Linda **have broken off** their engagement.

Last night a gunman **held up** a local bank and took four hostages.

Wait a moment while I **write out** a cheque.

Note: If the noun phrase (object) is very long, the second order is normally used.

He **bottled up** all his negative feelings about his mother-in-law until he could stand it no longer.

If the object is a pronoun, only the first order is possible.

verb + object pronoun + particle

They've had to **put** it **off** till next week. (NOT ~~put off it.~~)

I'm trying to **sort** it **out**. (NOT ~~sort out it~~)

It's your problem; you'll have to **work** it **out** on your own. (NOT ~~work out it~~)

Type 3: two particles

verb + particle + particle + object In this type of phrasal verb the particles are not separable.

I find it hard to **put up with** all this noise.

I've always **looked up to** my father.

He **got away with** cold-blooded murder.

Note: If the verb is in the passive, you can't separate the verb and the particle.

The shop **was taken over** by a large supermarket chain.

The waters of the river **have been used up** by various industrial enterprises.

The same is true of questions: you can't normally separate the particle from the verb.

What **are** you **laughing at**? (NOT ~~At what are you laughing~~?)

1 (2) Practice

The following phrasal verbs are used in this unit. Check their meaning, using a dictionary if necessary.

Type 1: not separable

come across	count on	deal with	do without
flick through	get over	look into	look through

Type 2: separable

bottle up　bring up　cross out　do up　fill in
get down　hand in　look up　pick up　print out
put across　shut down　sort out　talk through
tell apart　think through　throw away

Type 3: two particles

catch up with　come up with　get back to
look forward to　put up with

1 Complete the sentences with the noun and the phrasal verb given in *italics*. Sometimes there are two possibilities.

a) I'll be with you in a minute. I just want to flick through the paper first.
the paper / flick through

b) I don't think he put his ideas across or put across his ideas very well at all.
his ideas / put across

c) I'll ______________________
for you if you don't have enough time.
train times / look into

d) We really need to ______________
as soon as possible. *things / talk through*

e) Could you ______________________
on your way here? *a bottle of wine / pick up*

f) If you've got a minute, could you
______________________ and tell me
what you think. *this report / look through*

g) You can always ______________________
to be the last to arrive! *Sarah / count on*

h) Let me know if you ______________________
anywhere, will you? *my mobile / come across*

i) It's important to talk. You really shouldn't
______________________ you know.
your feelings / bottle up

j) First we're going to ______________________
and then we're going to ______________________
______________________ *the garden / sort out*
the inside of the house / do up

2 Complete the sentences using the phrasal verbs in the box and an appropriate pronoun (me, them, it etc).

~~bring up~~　come across　cross out　deal with
do without　fill in　flick through　get down
~~get over~~　hand in　look up　print out
shut down　tell apart　throw away

a) I know he's a bit disappointed about it now, but I'm sure he'll get over it soon.

b) If you feel strongly about the changes to working hours, bring them up at the next meeting.

c) If you make a mistake, just ______________
neatly.

d) If the computer freezes, ______________,
leave it for a minute or so and then reboot it.

e) I didn't read the whole book. I just
______________ quickly.

f) Do you ever read these old magazines? If not,
I'm going to ______________

g) It's difficult to ______________ – they look
almost identical.

h) If you've got a problem at work, you really ought
to ______________ as soon as possible.

i) I'll show you the photos as soon as I
____

j) If you don't know what it means,
______________ in the dictionary.

k) My personal assistant is invaluable. I couldn't
______________ for one minute.

l) I've lost my car keys. Let me know if you
____

m) I've had enough of this rain. It's really starting
to ______________

n) You need to get form M99, ______________,
and then ______________ to the office.

3 Complete the e-mail with the two-particle phrasal verbs in the box at the top of the page.

Hi Jim,

It was good to see you the other day and (a)______________ all your news. And sorry again to hear about your new boss – I don't know how you (b)______________ it. Anyway, let's try and (c)______________ a date for dinner soon – I'll check my diary and (d)______________ you in the next few days. I (e)______________ it.

Best, Graham

2 Taste (1)

Describing nouns

The noun phrase

A noun phrase always includes a noun, but it may also have words and structures that give you more information about the noun.

The following all come before the noun.

determiners: *a, the, some, any, this, those, his, my, few, many, enough, several, this, those*

adjectives: *dark, big, new, important, financial, technical, amused, interested, general, available, modern, absolute*

numbers: *three, thirty-three, one million*

nouns used like adjectives to modify other nouns: *car (door), country (road) cat (food), surprise (announcement).* Almost any noun can be used in this way.

Descriptive details

These come after the noun. A description after a noun can be:

- **a prepositional phrase** (preposition + noun phrase)
  the boy **at the back of the class**
  a man **with a violent temper**
  strong feelings **of jealousy**
  my view **from the window**
- **a relative clause** (with or without a relative pronoun)
  the man **who came into the room**
  the street **where you live**
  the mobile phone **that I bought yesterday**
  all the people **I know**
- **a present participle clause**
  the dog **lying under the table.**
  people **working in the public sector**
  a flock of birds **flying high in the sky**
  a girl **sitting on the grass**
- **a past participle clause**
  a girl **called Mandy**
  the landscape **seen from the train**
  a member of parliament **elected by the people**
  the restaurant **recommended by the Michelin guide**
- **a *to*-infinitive clause**
  his failure **to get along with his classmates**
  her ability **to read at the age of four**
  a device **to measure the alcohol level in the blood**
  the resources **to build a good team**
- **an adjective clause**
  the people **responsible for the project**
  the facilities **available here**
  the weapons **likely to be used in the attack**
  a manager **capable of inspiring the players**

Many noun phrases have determiners, adjectives etc. before the main noun and descriptive details after it. Here the main noun is *hotel.*

I stayed in **a small family-run** hotel **outside the village**.

Order of adjectives

When you use more than one adjective before a noun, the usual order is: **opinion adjective; 'size' adjective; colour adjective; 'fact' adjective**. ('Fact' adjectives put the noun in a particular class.)

a **beautiful little Japanese** car
rapid technological advance
a **large black circular** table
blue Venetian glass

When a noun is used to modify an adjective, it comes immediately before the main noun, after all other adjectives.

a **successful American software** company
the **flourishing Indian film** industry

Comparative and superlative adjectives normally come in front of all other adjectives.

bigger commercial sea-going boats
the **prettiest little old** cottage in the village

2 (1) Practice

1 Underline the adjectives, nouns, prepositional phrases, relative and participle clauses that describe the **nouns** in **bold**.

a) I was staying in a rundown old **farmhouse** surrounded by vineyards.

b) It was at the end of a long twisting country **road**, about ten minutes' drive from the nearest **village**.

c) The only **source of heat** in the house was the constantly-burning log **fire** in each room.

d) Out of my two tiny second-floor **windows** I could see mile after mile of leafy **vineyards** stretching into the distance.

e) The home-cooked **meals** they served were perhaps among the very best **cooking** I've ever tasted.

f) Each meal was accompanied by a glass or two of local **wine**.

g) The **music** played in the restaurant was an interesting **mixture** of traditional and modern.

2 Rewrite the sentences, putting the words and phrases in *italics* into an appropriate position in the sentence.

a) We rented a villa. *small; situated just outside the resort; with a swimming pool.*

b) We visited this temple. *little; decorated with hundreds of flags; lovely; Buddhist*

c) There were palm trees. *swaying in the breeze; tall; rows of*

d) We're going to see that film. *you were going on about; French; old*

e) I'm going to get mp3 players. *next-generation; one of those; advertised on TV.*

f) I work in that building. *next to the bus station; grey; with the big clock; ugly*

3 Put the words given into the correct order.

a) I live in / flat / the city centre / not far from / a / small

b) stretching for miles / of my bedroom / fields / green / lots of / out of the window / I can see

c) by the sea / I really need / a / holiday / relaxing

d) with internet and mp3 / those / one of / mobile phones / new / I've got / trendy

e) 1980s / I've got / brilliant / heavy metal bands / CDs / by / loads of

4 Describe the following. If possible, use at least one determiner, adjective, prepositional phrase and/or relative clause for each. For example, *I'm wearing a pair of black denim jeans I got for my birthday.*

a) the building you are in

b) something you're wearing

c) your favourite possession

d) your favourite place

e) your favourite food

2 *Taste (2)*

Fronting

Normally, in English, a sentence begins with the subject. But you can use **fronting** to bring some other element forward into a position before the subject. Fronting is often used for dramatic effect in narratives.

Fronting with subject-verb inversion

Sometimes when you use fronting there is **subject-verb inversion**; the verb comes before the subject.

- In most cases it is an adverbial that is fronted before the subject-verb inversion.

Usual word order (subject + verb + adverbial)	**Fronting** (adverbial + verb + subject)
A little old man sat on a stool in a dark corner.	On a stool in a dark corner **sat a little old man**.
The family lived on the upper floors.	On the upper floors **lived the family**.
Then **the rain came** down.	Down **came the rain**.

- Sometimes it is the complement that is fronted before the subject-verb inversion.

The view over the valley **was particularly spectacular**.	**Particularly spectacular was** the view over the valley.
The grief of the child's parents **was equally distressing**.	**Equally distressing was** the grief of the child's parents.

You often do this when the complement is a comparative adjective.
The main course was good, but **even better was the dessert that followed**.

You can also front the past participle *gone* and invert the subject and verb; in these sentences *gone* is used adjectivally.

The days of summer sunshine are gone.	Gone **are the days of summer sunshine**.

When direct speech or thought is represented, the subject and reporting verb can be inverted.
'What is going to happen to me now?' **wondered Bill**, worriedly.

Note: If the subject is a pronoun, you do not usually invert the subject and the verb.

Up onto her feet **she jumped** and hurried back to her room (NOT ~~Up onto her feet jumped she~~…)

This type of fronting, with subject-verb inversion, is normally used in writing. But some uses of inversion are common in everyday speech, especially with *here, there, first, next, then,* and *now,* and the verbs *be, come* and *go*.

Here**'s your dinner**.	Here **comes the rain**.
There **goes the last tram**.	First **came the oral exam**.
Next **was the reading test**.	Then **came the listening test**.
Now **comes the tricky part**.	

Fronting with normal subject-verb order

You often front an adverbial without changing the order of subject and verb.

The ferry was **often** delayed by bad weather.	**Often** the ferry was delayed by bad weather.
Quiet fell **across the gathering of spectators**.	**Across the gathering of spectators** quiet fell.
She came **down the great wide wooden staircase**.	**Down the great wide wooden staircase** she came.

You can also front an object or complement without changing the order of subject and verb.

I shall ignore **his rudeness**.	**His rudeness** I shall ignore.
A computer could solve **most of these problems**.	**Most of these problems** a computer could solve.

You often do this in spoken English, where the object or complement is what strikes the speaker first, and the main point about it comes at the end. You can put a comma after the object or complement.
Siegfried, I think his name is.

Sometimes the object is repeated, as a pronoun, in the normal place in the sentence.
My little son Billy, I absolutely adore **him**.

2 (2) Practice

1 Underline all the examples of fronting in these book extracts.

a) Quiet fell once again across the gathering, but it was of a different, more menacing kind. Gone was the silence of conspiracy, replaced by oppressive guilt.

b) On the walls, now, hung simple rural landscapes. Gone were the colourful historical scenes that had been so much in favour with the Hung Mao. Gone were the lavish screens and bright floral displays of former days.

c) Long have I combed the vilest quarters of this town on a fruitless search for thee. From wharf to palazzo have I searched.

2 Complete these newspaper extracts with the words given to show fronting.

a) German international Steffen Freund went down

> Down went German international Steffen Freund, but referee Mike Riley was not impressed and waved play on.

b) Morton stepped up

> Five minutes into the second half, the home side needlessly gave away a free kick on the edge of their own penalty box. ______________ and drilled it low into the corner to make it 1–1.

c) I went along

> I was assured by my specialist that the wait would not be long. So ______________ to the hospital and sat and suffered with all the others, waiting and waiting for an interminable length of time.

d) The staid white trousers and red jackets were gone

> We finally got a glimpse of the new-look uniform. ______________, replaced by slim-fitting, modern red suits.

e) The president walked across the room

> ______________ to rapturous applause from even his most ardent of critics.

3 Each of these book extracts originally contained an example of fronting. Identify where this was and restore it to its original form. You do not need to write out the whole text, just the section containing the fronting.

a) That morning, at the start of January, he felt no desire except to remain in bed. The guilt he used to experience whenever he took a day off work was gone.

Gone was the guilt he used to experience whenever he took at day off work.

b) Now they were running along a gloomy passageway, to a room at the very end. The children flew through the door, into a dark room whose windows were boarded up.

____

c) His hand shot up in a flash. He was desperately hoping the teacher would choose him to answer the question.

____

d) The sound of singing from the distant church came through the open window. Sasha stopped and listened.

____

4 Rephrase the sentences beginning with the word given.

a) Andrew is coming.
Here comes Andrew.

b) It's starting to rain.
Here ______________

c) The interesting bit is next.
Next ______________

d) The bus is here.
Here ______________

e) Look – Harry is going.
Look – there ______________

f) The intelligence tests came first.
First ______________

g) The interview was at the end of the day.
At the end of the day ______________

3 City (1)

Hedging

Sometimes you do not want to state a fact too categorically as you are not sure that you can prove that it is true. You can use a range of expressions to distance yourself from facts and opinions. This is called **hedging**.

Hedging with verbs

You can use *appear* and *seem* to create a distance between yourself and what is said. These verbs are followed either by a *that* clause or a *to*-infinitive.

It **seems (that)** the President may soon stand down.

It **seems (that)** there has been a generally favourable reaction to the proposals.

The outcome **seems to be** inevitable.

It **appears (that)** the story was deliberately leaked to the press by the government.

The weather **appears to be changing**.

The sleeping arrangements **appeared to be** satisfactory.

To add further distance you can use the modal *would*.

It **would seem (that)** there is nothing else we can do.

It **would appear (that)** you have already made up your minds.

You **would appear to have made** an unwise decision.

You can use *it looks as if*, *it looks as though*, and *it looks like* to distance yourself.

It **looks as if** they might not need our help any longer.

It **looks as though** the situation is getting worse.

It **looks like** the prime minister is getting further involved in the scandal.

Hedging with the passive voice

You can use the passive to avoid expressing an opinion as your own, for example because you want to present the opinion as something generally believed, rather than your own personal belief.

It **is** generally **recognized** that our electoral system is in need of reform.

It **cannot be denied** that standards of living are deteriorating.

It **has** often **been claimed** that lifestyle has a greater impact on health than nutrition.

There **are not believed** to be any survivors.

Life in the country **is** widely **thought** to be healthier than life in the city.

It **is not known** whether he will accept the offer.

This use is fairly formal and is often used in news reports.

Hedging using *there is* & *there are*

You can also use clauses beginning with *there is* or *there are*, followed by a noun like *doubt* or *evidence*.

There is little doubt that the election was rigged.

There is some doubt that the change of government will bring any real progress.

There is no doubt that the government has been effective in controlling inflation.

There is little evidence of any change.

There is little evidence that people in general are better off than they were five years ago.

You can add further distance by using *can*.

There can be little doubt that the election was rigged.

There can be no doubt that the government has been effective in controlling inflation.

You can combine different hedging devices.

There would appear to be little doubt that the election was rigged.

3 (1) Practice

1 Rewrite the sentences in two different ways using the verb in *italics* and beginning with the words given.

a) The shop has closed down. *appear*
The shop appears to have closed down.
It appears that the shop has closed down.

b) There's been a mistake. *appear*
There ______
It ______

c) They've been delayed. *would appear*
They ______
It ______

d) He's left. *seem*
He ______
It ______

e) We are in a bit of a mess. *would seem*
We ______
It ______

2 The most common and useful verb for hedging is *seem*. Rewrite the sentences using *seem* + infinitive.

a) I've lost my key.
I seem to have lost my key.

b) The internet isn't working.
______

c) There's a mistake with the bill.
______

d) We've been overcharged.
______

e) There's no hot water.
______

f) The bar isn't open yet.
______

g) Nobody speaks English.
______

h) He's upset about something.
______

3 Make the statements more impersonal using the passive voice.

a) You told us you'd accepted the offer.
It was understood you'd accepted the offer.

b) We assumed you were going to book the tickets.
______

c) Didn't we decide that you'd do the driving?
______?

d) We agreed we'd all help out, didn't we?
______?

4 Complete the news story with a passive voice structure that includes the word(s) in brackets. Use *it* or *there* where necessary.

(a) ______ (believe) that London has become the billionaire capital of the world. (b) ______ (now / think) to be more billionaires living in London than in any other city. Convenient travel to other European cities and the USA (c) ______ (understand) to be the major factor. (d) ______ (also / report) that London is now the first choice for senior executives when deciding where to locate any new European-based business.

5 Report the newspaper headlines in a natural way beginning with the words given.

a) **President set to resign**
It looks like the president is going to resign.

b) **Wade Moony set to miss World Cup**
It looks as if ______
______

c) **Playing computer games increases brainpower**
It appears ______
______

d) **Vegetarian diet can add five years to your life**
It seems ______
______

e) **Next summer set to be hottest on record**
It looks as though ______
______

f) **Does new anti-ageing drug work?**
There is some doubt ______
______

g) **'Alien' photos proved genuine**
There is no doubt ______
______

h) **Hurricane leaves 50 000 homeless**
It's now thought ______
______

i) **Harry and Tara to wed**
It's rumoured ______
______

3 City (2)

Negative & limiting adverbials

Sometimes you can place a negative or limiting adverbial in the front position in a sentence to create emphasis. You do this especially in formal or written contexts.

Word order

In this type of sentence, the subject and auxiliary or modal are inverted. The sentence begins with the adverbial.

I have never seen anything quite so breathtaking. Never **have I** seen anything quite so breathtaking.

The same thing happens with the verb *be:* the subject and the verb are inverted.

It is not only one of the oldest cities on Earth, but also one of the most beautiful.

Not only **is it** one of the oldest cities on Earth, it is also one of the most beautiful.

In the present simple and past simple, you use the auxiliary *do/does* or *did*.

We rarely **visit** that part of town. Rarely **do we visit** that part of town.

Negative adverbials

***Not a* + noun**

Not a word **did she** say to anyone. Not a sound **did they** hear.

Not until

Not until he arrived at his destination **did he** discover the letter hidden in his luggage.

Not until the day before our departure **were we** told about the change in the itinerary.

Under no circumstances

Under no circumstances **can deposits** be refunded after the date of departure.

On no account

On no account **must this door** be left unlocked. On no account **can you** smoke in the house.

Never (before/again)

Never before **had I** seen anything so breathtakingly beautiful.

No sooner...than

No sooner **had we** set off than the bus ground to a halt.

Not only...but

Not only **did we** lose our money, but we had to walk home.

Limiting adverbials

Only

Only by complaining to the manager in person **did I** manage to get the hotel room properly cleaned.

Only if he promised to help **would she** tell him where he had left his keys.

Only after they had finished their lunch **were they** allowed outside to play.

Little

Little **did they** know that we were following them.

Rarely/seldom

Rarely / seldom **do I** visit a city more than once, but this place is really special.

Hardly/barely...when

Hardly / barely **had we** arrived when there was a knock at the door.

3 (2) Practice

1 (Circle) the negative and limiting adverbials in the following quotations. Underline where the subject + auxiliary word order is inverted.

a) (...never) have I seen destruction, panic and fear on this massive scale. (Jo Bonner, US Congressman, talking about the aftermath of Hurricane Katrina)

b) Never, never and never again shall it be that this beautiful land will again experience the oppression of one by another. (Nelson Mandela, South African President)

c) Only by great risks can great results be achieved. (Xerxes, Persian king)

d) Not until we are lost do we begin to understand ourselves. (Henry David Thoreau, US philosopher)

e) Rarely have so many people been so wrong about so much. Never have the consequences of their misunderstanding been so tragic. (Richard Nixon, US president, on the Vietnam war)

f) Only if you have been in the deepest valley can you ever know how magnificent it is to be on the highest mountain. (Richard Nixon, US president, in his farewell address)

g) Rarely do great beauty and great virtue dwell together. (Petrarch, fourteenth-century Italian poet)

h) Never before had a woman put such agonizing poetry on canvas as Frida did at this time in Detroit. (Diego Riviera, Mexican artist, talking about his wife, painter Frida Kahlo)

i) Not only do I knock 'em out, I pick the round. (Mohammed Ali, boxer)

2 Complete the following extracts from newspaper articles with the negative and limiting adverbials in the box.

at no time	in no other	only when
never before	not before	not only
~~not until~~	only once in a generation	
seldom	under no circumstances	little

a) Not until he arrived on the 18th tee one shot behind did it suddenly occur to him that he was on the point of losing.

b) The demonstration continued unabated for eight hours and ________ police sprayed about 20 000 gallons of water into the crowds did the protesters finally disperse.

c) Two 14-year-old girls face manslaughter charges in a case that has stunned the western city of Calgary. ________ in the city have girls so young been charged with a killing.

d) The word from the White House is that ________ will the president admit he lied under oath to a federal grand jury. And that ________ will his mind be changed on this.

e) ________ is there a publishing phenomenon, which captures the world's imagination in the way Harry Potter has.

f) ________ he had delighted the audience for more than three hours did he finally leave the stage.

g) As he reeled away in celebration, ________ did he know that his 49th goal for his country was also to be his last.

h) ________ sport do so few spectators turn out to watch such highly paid sportsmen and women.

i) While economists are notorious for disagreeing among themselves, ________ has a single issue sparked more divergent views than the Euro has.

j) ________ is Windows itself configurable, but most of the applications that we use under Windows can also be tailored to your own tastes.

3 Rewrite the sentences beginning with a negative or limiting adverbial.

a) We will defeat this government only by being united.

____

____

b) You mustn't leave the exam hall with the paper under any circumstances.

____

____

c) The parts come packed in boxes so they very rarely get damaged.
The parts come packed in boxes so ________

____

d) I had no sooner got on the plane than I felt tears rolling down my face. I was not only leaving a special place, but also my family and friends.

____

____

____

4 Talk

Tendencies

You can use the modal *will* to talk about tendencies in general, and *would* to talk about tendencies in the past.

General tendencies

When you want to talk about facts that are generally true you use the present simple.

The Earth **revolves** around the sun.

The sun **rises** in the east and **sets** in the west.

The UK **consists** of four nations: England, Scotland, Wales and Northern Ireland.

Water **boils** at 100 degrees centigrade.

When you want to talk about things that generally tend to happen, without suggesting that they always, inevitably happen, you can use the modal *will ('ll)* or *will not (won't).*

Men **will** often prefer to talk about sports or the news, whilst women **will** talk about their relationships.

My neighbour **will** chat happily for hours about nothing in particular.

He**'ll go on** and on; there's no stopping him.

He **won't** always tell you when he's going to be home late.

And then when he does come home, he**'ll put** his feet **up** and sit there waiting for his dinner.

You can also use *will ('ll)* and *will not (won't)* in continuous or perfect forms.

If you go in the pub any evening, he**'ll be sitting** there with a drink in his hand.

You can tell her something one minute and she**'ll have forgotten** it the next.

No matter how late you arrive, you can guarantee that he **won't have got** ready to leave.

Note: You do not normally use *will* with this meaning in questions.

Tendencies in the past

You can use *would ('d)* to talk about habits, tendencies or characteristic behaviour in the past. You do not usually use this in the negative or in questions.

When I was young my father **would sit down** with me in the kitchen every day after school and help me with my homework. On Saturday mornings we **would go** to the movies together and he **would let** me go to the sweet shop on the way home. When we got back to the house my mother **would be** there and we **would** all **have** lunch together.

You can also use *would ('d)* in continuous or perfect forms.

When we got back to the house, my mother **would be waiting** for us.

Most afternoons she**'d be sitting** in her garden, talking to passers-by.

Whenever we arrived, they**'d have prepared** a big meal for us.

They**'d have been working** hard in the kitchen to cook exactly what we liked best.

For a single, specific event in the past, you use the past simple, not *would.*

My father **helped** me with my homework last night.

We **saw** a great film at the cinema last weekend.

Adverbials

You often use adverbials of frequency with these structures. Some of these are *always, often, usually, occasionally, from time to time* and *once in a blue moon.*

She will (she'll) **often** stop to talk to me on my way home from school.

She will **occasionally** go out for a meal or to see a movie, but **usually** she will just stay home and watch television.

She would cook a meal **once in a blue moon** – mostly we ate takeaways or ready meals.

From time to time she would give me some sweets or biscuits and that would be my supper.

4 Practice

1 Complete the advice about public speaking using *will* and the verbs in the box.

be	end up	forgive	give	make
respond	sound	recall		

Avoid reading your speech

A speech or presentation delivered from notes of key words and ideas (a) __________ more natural and engaging. Don't read a script.

Get the audience involved

Audiences (b) _____ usually _____ very happy to participate in activities. And participants who have been involved (c) __________ more of the content of the talk afterwards. They (d) __________ more to requests that are made with confidence and not in a weak or embarrassed sort of way.

Don't appear rushed or anxious

Take your time. Avoid appearing rushed. If something goes wrong, don't panic and deal with it in a calm and professional manner. Remain composed and people (e) _____ almost always _____ you no matter what happens.

Speak at a natural rate

Speak the way you would in conversation. Speaking too fast (f) _____ generally _____ you appear nervous and it (g) __________ the impression that you want to get the talk over with as quickly as possible.

Make your speeches/presentations informal and conversational

'Formal' speeches and presentations (h) _____ often _____ sounding boring and uninspiring. Speak like you would in conversation. Just relax.

2 In the original version of the following text there were seven examples of where *will* or *won't* was used to express tendency instead of the present simple. Underline the present simple forms where this is possible and then write the alternatives with *will* or *won't*.

a) will often tell
b) ______________________
c) ______________________
d) ______________________
e) ______________________
f) ______________________
g) ______________________

People often tell you that being a student is one of the best times of your life. But as a student you most likely don't have a lot of money and a part-time job may be difficult to keep with the workload that you no doubt face. Accommodation is usually a student's biggest expense and there are a couple of things, which are very important to bear in mind when choosing where to live. You often find the cheapest accommodation within the school or college and failing that you can always live in a hostel or in a host family. Many schools and colleges have a network of local families they can recommend. Another possibility is sharing a flat with others, but remember this doesn't always suit everyone and it might not be worth the effort if you don't get on with each other too well.

3 In the original version of the following text there were six examples of where *would* or *wouldn't* was used instead of the past simple. Underline the past simple forms where this is possible and write the alternatives with *would* or *wouldn't*.

a) would go
b) ______________________
c) ______________________
d) ______________________
e) ______________________
f) ______________________

When I was a child, we went to the coast once a year to stay with my aunt and uncle, who had a house right on the beach. It was a magical place and we played from dawn to dusk. The only time we weren't so happy was when it started raining, and although tropical rain can be very impressive, it upset us that we had to stay indoors. But then, my mother always had some interesting games for us to play and it wasn't so bad. It has now been a very long time since we all last went to the beach. We all grew up and moved away and even though we still visited from time to time, it never had that same magic and sense of adventure as when we were children.

5 *Luck (1)*

Unreal conditionals

The 'if' clause (describing an unreal situation)

When you want to describe a past situation that is unreal, or imagine how a past situation might have been different, you backshift the verb in the 'if'clause.

The past simple backshifts to **past perfect**, and the past continuous backshifts to **past perfect continuous**.

What really happened (real past)	What might have happened (unreal past)
She **won** a small amount of money in the lottery.	If she **had won** the jackpot…
He **didn't do** anything to improve the situation.	If he **had done** something…
He **was driving** too fast when he had the accident.	If he **hadn't been driving** so fast…
She **wasn't paying** attention.	If she **had been paying** attention…

Instead of using *if* to introduce the unreal situation, you can invert the subject and the auxiliary verb *had*. This structure is rather formal, and is more commonly used in writing.

If she **had won** the jackpot…	**Had she** won the jackpot…
If **we'd** known earlier...	**Had we** known earlier…
If **your work had** been more satisfactory…	**Had your work** been more satisfactory…

Note: If the sentence is negative, the word *not* comes after the subject.

Had you not been so silly… (NOT ~~Had not you been so silly~~…)

Note: In informal spoken English, some people use *'d have* and *hadn't have* in 'if' clauses referring to the past. This is often considered incorrect, and it would be better for you not to use it.

If **I'd have known**, I would have been more careful.

If he **hadn't have delivered** my pizza that night, I'd never have met him.

The main clause

Describing possible present consequences

You use *would* + infinitive, or *would* + present continuous infinitive (*be* + *-ing*) to describe the possible present consequences of an unreal past situation.

If I had trusted him to help me in my career, I **would be** rich and famous by now.

If she had been paying more attention, she **wouldn't be** in such a mess.

If you hadn't sacked me for no reason, **I'd be running** the company now.

If she had won the lottery, she **wouldn't be working** in the factory any longer

Describing possible past consequences

You use *would* or *wouldn't* and the perfect infinitive (*have* + past participle) or the perfect continuous infinitive (*have* + *been* + present participle *-ing*) to describe the possible past consequences of an unreal past situation.

If she had won the lottery she **would have bought** a snazzy red sports car.

If you had listened to me, you **wouldn't have made** so many mistakes.

If we hadn't been so careful about choosing the hotel, we**'d** probably **have been overlooking** a building site.

If the lesson had been a little more interesting, she **wouldn't have been daydreaming** in class.

You can also use *could* or *might* in the main clause.

If anybody had asked me, I **could have told** them what happened.

If you had asked me for help, I **might have been** able to do something before it was too late.

Note: You can put the main clause and the 'if' clause in either order. When you put the main clause first, there is usually no comma between the clauses.

She wouldn't have been daydreaming in class if the lesson had been a little more interesting.

5 (1) Practice

1 Write conditional sentences using the prompts.

a) I didn't have enough time → I couldn't help them
If I'd had more time, I could've helped them.

b) you weren't listening → you don't know what to do

____

c) I didn't have your e-mail address → I couldn't send you the photos

____

d) you stayed up all night → you're feeling tired

____

e) he didn't know about the party → he didn't go

____

f) I wasn't thinking straight → I told Harry about Anna

____

g) you rushed into things → you are in this mess

____

h) I didn't know what was going on → I didn't stay

____

2 Complete the extracts with the words in the box.

not confront/only have to	run/won	be/be	invest/now be/take	~~know/stop~~	play/not murder	quit/might change

a) The defendant said that he was scared and that he thought someone was going to attack him. 'That's why I ran away,' he told the court. 'If I __had known__ they were police, I __would have stopped__. They weren't in uniform.'

b) Navratilova finally retired from singles, having won 18 Grand Slams singles titles, including a record nine Wimbledon crowns. 'If I ________ at 30, I ________ my mind and made ill-judged comebacks, but I quit at 38,' she said, 'when I knew I'd done my part.'

c) 'I saw on the TV replays that Jones ran out of her lane, which means she ran about two metres less than everybody else in the race,' Ottey said, before conceding that even if Jones ________ in her lane she still probably ________ the race.

d) Evans had to struggle against the current to drag Ross to the bank and haul him clear of the water. Ross's mother, Sheena, praised her son's rescuer saying 'If it ________ for Mark's bravery, my son ________ alive now.'

e) If we ________ the regime about the alleged atrocities when we did last month, we ________ do so at some later stage, in circumstances much more dangerous for their neighbours and the rest of the world.

f) Who knows what music John Lennon ________ today if he ________ in 1980.

g) The best unit trust over all sectors over the last five years was the GA North American Growth fund. If you ________ $1000 over that period, it ________ worth $3,180 and you would ________ your adviser out for dinner.

3 Rewrite the conditional sentences beginning with *Had*.

a) If I'd known, I wouldn't have said anything.

____

b) If it hadn't been for Jim, we'd be a right mess now.

____

c) If things had been different, I might never have gone to university at all.

____

d) If you'd got here a bit earlier, you'd have seen for yourself.

____

5 Luck (2)

Wishes & regrets

Talking about regrets using *I wish*

You backshift the verb after *wish* to express the following unreal (and wished for) situations. You often omit *that* after *I wish*.

Regrets about past situations

I **left** early.	I wish that I **hadn't left** so early.
I **didn't tell** you the truth.	I wish I**'d told** you the truth.
I **wasn't** really **concentrating**.	I wish I**'d been concentrating**.

Regrets about the present

I **don't have** enough time to study.	I wish that I **had** more time to study.
You**'re working** very hard at the moment.	I wish you **weren't working** so hard.

A desire to change the future

They**'re coming** to visit us next weekend.	I wish that they **weren't coming** to visit us next weekend.
I**'m going to fail** my exam again.	I wish I **wasn't going to fail** my exam again.

You can also use *could* to emphasize your inability to change a situation in the present or future.

I wish that I **could understand** these instructions.

I wish I **could come** to the party tonight.

You can also use *would ('d)* to describe a desired change in the present or future. It emphasizes a sense of longing or irritation.

It never **rains** in this country.	I wish that it **would rain**.
You **aren't paying** attention.	I wish you**'d pay** attention.
It's after midnight and he**'s playing** the piano.	I wish he **wouldn't play** the piano so late at night.
You **smoke** in the house.	I wish you **wouldn't smoke** in the house.

Other ways of expressing regret

***If only* + past perfect**

If only we**'d known**.

If only the weather **hadn't been** so awful.

***Regret* + *-ing* & *regret* + perfect participle**

I **regret choosing** French when I was at school.

I **regret not having practised** the piano more when I was young.

I **regret having been forced** to leave school at the age of 16. (passive)

The structure with the perfect participle is more formal.

Wish + *to*-infinitive

You can use *wish* + *to*-infinitive to express a formal intention, especially in writing.

We **wish to inform** you that the offices will be closed on Mondays until further notice.

We **wish to congratulate** you on your recent success.

I **wish to thank** the committee for their support.

If you **wish to comment** on our services, please write to the following address.

***Regret* + *to*-infinitive**

You can also use *regret* + *to*-infinitive in a formal context to say that you are sorry about something. This structure is often used to break bad news.

We **regret to announce** that all trains are subject to delay due to bad weather.

5 (2) Practice

1 Complete these newspaper extracts by putting the verb into the most natural form.

a) The material side of Ms Rowling's rags to riches success has yet to permeate. Friendly and confiding, she bubbles over with conversation and wit. Her publishers may sometimes wish she ______________ (be) less forthcoming, but her openness is part of her restless charm.

b) Rooney was one of several players that had a crack at the ball as it repeatedly rolled loose in West Ham's penalty area, but the goal didn't come. 'It's one of those moments you wish you ______________ (play),' manager Ferguson said.

c) Smith was offered a place to read politics, philosophy and economics at Magdalen College, Oxford, but he decided to read English instead. 'I now wish I ______________ (do) PPE after all,' he told me.

d) This movie is simply dreadful. You watch it and wish you ______________ (have) amnesia.

e) 'It was a fantastic match and I felt totally in control throughout the last two sets,' Henman said, 'I just wish I ______________ (can play) like that every game.'

f) More than 50 US and international news organizations have descended on Jasper for the trial. 'We just wish this trial ______________ (end) so we can get back to our daily lives,' said local resident Jim Woods.

g) Outside the courtroom, Adams spoke to waiting reporters. 'I wish my critics ______________ (wait) to find out the real position before they reached such hasty judgments,' he said, 'It is behind me now and I just wish ______________ (get on with) rebuilding my life and political career.'

2 For each situation write a wish or regret beginning with the words given.

a) I drank too much.
I wish I hadn't drunk so much.

b) I really shouldn't have said that.
I really regret ______________

c) I didn't speak to her when I had the chance.
I wish ______________

d) I didn't realize she'd be so upset.
If only ______________

e) I hope it stops raining soon.
I wish ______________

f) I didn't take it seriously enough.
I regret ______________

g) I've got too much work on at the moment.
I wish ______________

h) I'm going out tonight.
I wish ______________

3 Complete the extracts using *regret* and an appropriate form of the verbs in the box, *-ing* or *to*-infinitive.

announce	inform	~~offer~~	say	take

a) You probably regret offering to help now but I promise I won't pester you more than is absolutely necessary!

b) I ______________ you that the board turned down your proposal.

c) Despite having lost, Ms Radin does not ______________ the case to court.

d) 'Ladies and gentlemen, we ______________ that, due to an accident to Mr Banks, we will be unable to continue with tonight's performance.'

e) I ______________ a lot of things in my life, but what I said this morning is definitely not one of them.

4 Complete the letter extracts using *wish* and the verbs in the box.

comment	deposit	take

a) Our manager will give personal attention to your enquiry and point you in the right direction if you ______________ the matter further.

b) If members of the public or organizations ______________ on this matter, they should write to Road Accident Casualties in Lothian Region.

c) If you ______________ money outside banking ours using the CreditPoint service, then you must use a LloydsTSB CreditPoint envelope provided by the Bank.

6 Mind (1)

Verbs of the senses

You can talk about your senses (sight, hearing, feeling, smell and taste) in two ways:

- using stative verbs, to refer to abilities or sensations: *see, hear, feel, smell, taste*
- using dynamic verbs, to refer to voluntary actions: *look (at)/watch, listen (to), touch/feel, smell, taste*

Stative If you **see** smoke, run.

Stative I **didn't hear** anything...

Dynamic **Watch** carefully while I show you how this works.

Dynamic ...although I **was listening** carefully.

Can, could & be able to

You often use *can, could* or *be able to* with stative verbs of the senses.

I **could hear** voices, but I **couldn't see** anyone.

I **could smell** the smoke, but I **couldn't see** the fire.

I would love to **be able to hear** as well as I **could** when I was younger.

I put loads of garlic in this soup, but I **can** hardly **taste** it at all.

Continuous forms

Verbs with stative meanings are rarely used in continuous forms. Some verbs, however, can be used in either a stative or a dynamic way, i.e. in simple or continuous tenses, with a change in meaning.

Look over there – what **do** you **see**?/what **can** you **see**? (NOT ~~what are you seeing~~)
When **are** you **seeing** Tom? (= meeting)

I **can hear** someone coming upstairs. (NOT ~~I'm hearing~~)
I'm sure we**'ll be hearing** a lot more about this new technology in the coming year. (= be told about it)

I **felt** somebody push me from behind. (NOT ~~I was feeling~~)
I hope you**'re feeling** better now. (= talking about your state of health)

I've got a cold, so I **can't smell** anything properly. (NOT ~~I'm not smelling~~)
He**'s smelling** her new perfume. (= investigating)

Can you **taste** something funny in this wine? (NOT ~~are you tasting~~)
We**'d been tasting** different wines all week but that one was really something special. (= trying)

Other stative verbs

Verbs that are always stative

There are some verbs that are always stative and are never used in continuous tenses. Here are a few of them.

I **know** I won't get the job. (NOT ~~I'm knowing~~)
Put the phone back where it **belongs**. (NOT ~~it is belonging~~)
All the employees said they **prefer** flexible working hours. (NOT ~~they are preferring~~)
I **don't mind** the heat; in fact I quite enjoy it. (NOT ~~I'm not minding~~)
I **don't believe** a word of what you're saying. (NOT ~~I'm not believing~~)

Verbs with both stative and dynamic meanings

Some verbs can be used in either a stative or a dynamic way, with a change of meaning. According to the meaning, they can be used in either simple or continuous tenses.

I **think** this milk has gone bad.
She's a good teacher because she **has** a lot of patience.
What **do** you weigh?
Your new jacket **looks** pretty good.
He always **appears** calm.

What **are** you **thinking** about?
I **was** just **having** a look around.
He **was weighing** the vegetables at the checkout.
I **was looking** out of the window and thinking.
The new fashions **will be appearing** next spring.

6 (1) Practice

1 What are the people saying? Complete the following using *can* or *can't* and the words in the box.

not feel/my fingers	hear/a buzzing noise
~~not see/him~~ smell/gas	really taste/the garlic

a) I _can't see him._

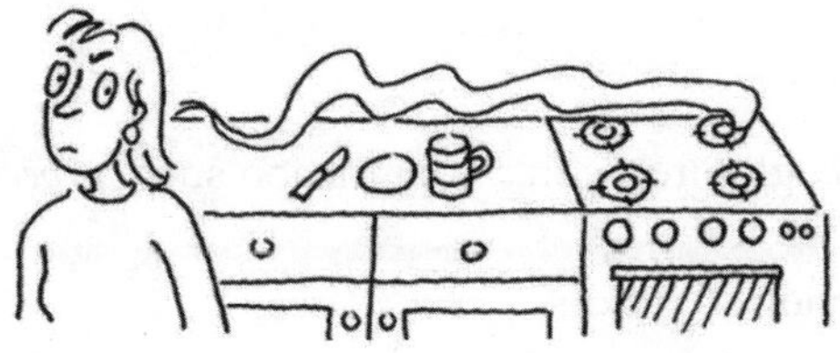

b) I ______________________________

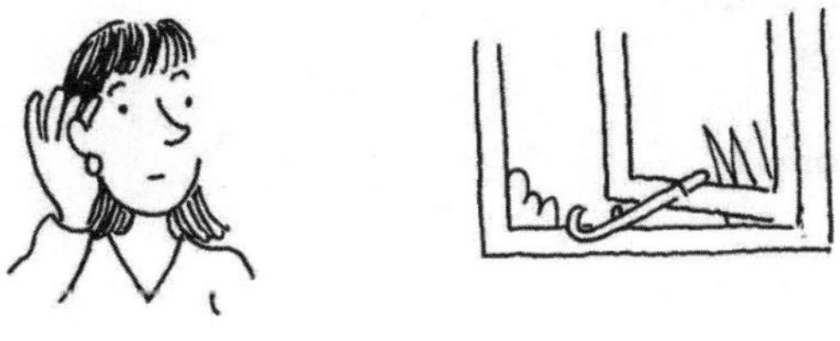

c) _____ you ______________________?

d) You ____________________________

e) I ______________________________

2 Complete the sentences using the verbs in the box.

belong/know	not mind/have/prefer
not know/have	taste/want
weigh/reckon/look	~~smell/think~~ think/think

a) This milk _smells_ a bit funny. I _think_ it's gone off.

b) I ______________ you ______________ a baby. Congratulations.

c) Mmm, this soup ______________ pretty good. _____ you __________ some?

d) My new mobile ______________ nothing – you don't even know it's in your pocket. And I ______________ it ______________ pretty cool too, don't you think?

e) ______ this bag ___________ to anyone? _______ anyone ___________ whose it might be?

f) I ______________ of getting a new car. I ______________ mine's on its last legs.

g) I ______________ what we ______________, Indian or Chinese – whatever you ____________

3 (Circle) the correct alternative.

A: (a) Who *do you look/are you looking* at?

B: (b) That guy over there. *Don't you think/Aren't you thinking* he *looks like/is looking like* Katie's ex?

A: (c) I *hear/am hearing* Jane had a party last night. It *sounds/is sounding* like it was great fun.

B: (d) Yes, great. I *was/was being* surprised not to see you there though.

A: (e) I *didn't know/wasn't knowing* anything about it.

B: (f) Oh, I *see/'m seeing*.

A: (g) I *just don't see/'m just not seeing* why I should apologize.

B: (h) Okay, suit yourself, but *I think/'m thinking* you *are/are being* totally unreasonable.

A: (i) I *seem/'m seeming* to have lost Sam's new mobile number. I don't *know/am not knowing* it – sorry.

B: (j) No problem. I *see/'m seeing* Tom later. I'm sure he*'ll have/'ll be having* it.

4 Complete the sentences so they are true for you. For example, *I don't see why there's so much fuss about football.*

a) I don't see ______________________
b) I'm seeing ______________________
c) It appears ______________________
d) I'm thinking ______________________
e) I think ______________________
f) I believe ______________________

6 *Mind (2)*

Participle clauses

Participle clauses do not include a subject or linking words. They can be formed with a present participle, a past participle or a perfect participle.

Present participle

Being a psychologist, she always thinks she knows what questions to ask.

Not having a lot of time, they decided to take a taxi.

Susie, **not wanting to interfere**, thought it wiser to say nothing at all.

Living in the country, they were used to relying on their own resources.

In the above sentences, the participle clause is equivalent to a clause beginning with a conjunction such as *because* or *as*. These are the equivalent sentences:

Because she's a psychologist, she always thinks she knows what questions to ask.

As they didn't have a lot of time, they decided to take a taxi.

Because Susie didn't want to interfere, she thought it wiser to say nothing at all.

As they lived in the country, they were used to relying on their own resources.

Past participle

Left together in the doctor's waiting room, they started a conversation.

Woken by the sound of breaking glass, James phoned the police.

Sarah, **not taken in by his charm**, refused his offer of dinner.

In the above sentences, the participle clause is equivalent to a clause in the passive voice. These are the equivalent sentences:

They were left together in the doctor's waiting room, so they started a conversation.

James was woken by the sound of breaking glass, so he phoned the police.

Sarah wasn't taken in by his charm, so she refused his offer of dinner.

Perfect participle (*having* + past participle)

Not having understood the question, she failed to answer it correctly.

Having mixed the chemicals together, we observed the reaction.

John, **not having been in hospital before**, didn't know what to expect.

Here the participle clause is equivalent to a clause beginning with a conjunction such as *because* or *after*. These are the equivalent sentences:

Because she hadn't understood the question, she failed to answer it correctly.

After we had mixed the chemicals together, we observed the reaction.

Because John hadn't been in hospital before, he didn't know what to expect.

Participle clauses beginning with a conjunction

A participle clause may also begin with a conjunction such as *when, while* or *after*.

While living in Paris, we met some famous writers and artists.

When challenged, he turned and ran away.

After having served three years in prison, he was released on parole.

Participle clauses after a noun

A present or past participle clause may also come after a noun. In this case, it is a type of defining relative clause giving more information about the noun.

She was carrying a basket **containing groceries**.

The food **served here** is expensive but very good.

6 (2) Practice

1 Complete the newspaper extracts by putting the verb in *italics* into an appropriate participle form.

a) Having spent large amounts of money on exploration and drilling, oil companies are quite keen to recoup their investment. *spend*

b) ________________ three goals up at half time, AC Milan must have thought they were 45 minutes away from the championship. Liverpool clearly had other ideas. *be*

c) ________________ all three substitutes, United faced an anxious last few minutes. *already use*

d) Clearly ________________ fully-fit, Beckham tended to pull up short of tackles and keep his running to an absolute minimum. *not be*

e) ________________ until next July, the latest Harry Potter adventure already has advanced orders of over one million in the UK alone. *not publish*

f) ________________ from the movie Titanic, 'My heart will go on' sold almost half a million copies in the first week of release. *take*

g) ________________ Sabatini before, Maleeva found she had to change tactics mid-game to keep her away from the net. *not play*

h) While ________________ the theft, the police came across evidence of further robberies. *investigate*

i) A bag ________________ high explosives was found during the raid. *contain*

2 Rewrite the sentences so the meaning is similar, beginning with a present or perfect participle clause.

a) I've walked all the way here so I'd quite like to sit down for a while.
Having walked all the way here, I'd quite like to sit down for a while.

b) Because I know what he's like, I'd rather not get involved.
____

c) Because I'm not American, I really don't understand the attraction of American football.
____

d) I've tried eating snails before, so I think I'll give it a miss if you don't mind.
____

e) We didn't know the area so we got completely lost.
____

f) I haven't met him, so I can't really comment.
____

g) I'm fluent in English and this makes it much easier for me to get work here.
____

h) Because I've never studied grammar, I don't really know the terminology.
____

i) John didn't know what to say , so he just stood there in silence.
John, ________________

3 The following book extracts originally began with a past participle clause. Restore them to their original form.

a) We were inspired with fresh hope so we hurried after him to find out more.
Inspired with fresh hope, we hurried after him to find out more.

b) She was taken by surprise so she could not answer for a moment.
____

c) We were woken by the dawn call and went to see the morning prayers at the Jama Masjid.
____

d) We were driven at great speed through the narrow streets of Old Delhi and watched the city come to life.
____

e) He was known affectionately as Dr Jock and he built up a tremendous rapport with his patients.
____

8 Cyberspace (1)

Will for predictions & assumptions

You can use *will* to show you are making a prediction.

(In the future) Computers **will** be more intelligent than humans.

You can also use *will* to make assumptions about the present or even the past.

(In the present) That**'ll** be David at the door. He said he'd call round about now.

(In the past) I imagine you **will** have learnt a lot by now.

Will ('ll) or *will not (won't)* + infinitive

Future predictions	In the future, people **will** certainly **live** longer.
	We definitely **won't travel** to other stars in the next century.
	Do you think genetic engineering **will be banned**? (passive)
Present assumptions	You've read *A Brief History of Time*, so you**'ll know** all about the origin of the universe.
	Sit down – you**'ll want** a rest after that long journey.
	You**'ll be** totally confident about using English on the phone by now.

Will ('ll) or *will not (won't)* + continuous

The passive voice (for example *will be being heard*) is extremely rare in this structure.

Future predictions	We**'ll** all **be working** from home by the end of the next century.
	We **won't be communicating** with aliens in the foreseeable future.
	How much longer **will** we **be using** cash as a means of payment?
Present assumptions	Don't phone them now – they**'ll be getting** ready to go out.
	You**'ll** either **be reading** this with a partner or **studying** it at home on your own.
	It's nine o'clock; he**'ll be sitting** in front of the TV now.

Will ('ll) or *won't (won't)* + perfect

Future predictions	By the end of this century we **will have learned** how to increase the size of the human brain.
	People say that the world's oil supplies **will have been used up** by the year 2050. (passive)
Present/past assumptions	You **won't have studied** English for very long I imagine.
	Look, there's an interesting article about Stephen Hawking here that you **won't have seen** yet.
Past assumptions	I suppose you**'ll have met** some interesting characters on your travels?
	You**'ll have taken** a holiday in an English-speaking country.

Will ('ll) or *will not (won't)* + perfect continuous

The passive voice (for example *will have been being heard*) is extremely rare in this structure.

Future predictions	They say the train's due in five minutes now – we**'ll have been waiting** 40 minutes
Present/past assumptions	We'd better phone them – they**'ll have been wondering** what's happened to us.
	You**'ll have been studying** in class and at home on your own.
Past assumptions	They came back with tons of stuff – they**'ll have been shopping** for hours.

Will + probably

Notice the position of *probably* in affirmative and negative sentences; usually it comes **after** *will* in affirmative sentences and **before** *won't* in negative sentences.

We'll **probably** learn to live in space stations.

We **probably** won't learn to live in space stations.

You'll **probably** have eaten already.

You **probably** won't have eaten already.

8 (1) Practice

1 Complete the text about the future of 'cyberspace' with the verbs in the box.

will be able	will be taking part
~~will not only have~~	will have become
will amass	will learn

By the end of the century, we (a) will not only have computers that (b) ________________ to communicate intelligently, but they (c) ________________ much more intelligent than we are. Via the internet they (d) ________________ in millions of 'conversations' simultaneously, in different languages, and with people and other computers all around the globe. In doing so, they (e) ________________ a great deal of second-hand experience, learning about human nature and our many flaws. In time, they (f) ________________ to control us.

2 Complete the web postings about the future of the internet using *will* and an appropriate form of the verbs in the box.

become	become	~~allow~~	forget

The capabilities of the internet (a) will allow for experiences so close to real life that the boundaries (b) ____________ blurred. People (c) ____________ addicted to virtual reality and in the not too distant future we (d) ____________ how to interact in the real world.
(Jim, San Francisco) Next posting

be	become	continue	create

The internet (e) ____________ infected by viruses and hackers and there (f) ____________ no security or privacy. Anti-virus companies (g) ____________ more viruses so they can sell their newest protections against them. Hackers (h) ____________ to break through 'secure' sites until nothing is secure or private.
(Ramos, Manilla) Next posting

look	look	read	recycle

Very soon we (i) ____________ all ____________ the same forwarded e-mails and (j) ____________ all at the same few websites, which (k) ____________ all ____________ and sound the same. Before we know it we (l) ____________ all ____________ the same material and information in a non-thinking, ever-shrinking cut-and-paste world.
(Dwayne, New York) Back to top

3 Write a prediction of your own about the future of the internet.

____

____

4 Rewrite the statements of facts as assumptions. Use *will* or *won't*.

a) That's Lauren on the phone.
That'll be Lauren on the phone.

b) Molly isn't back from work.
____

c) Russell hasn't arrived yet.
____

d) Come on! Kim is getting fed up with waiting for us.
____

e) Steve isn't feeling too happy about what she said.
____

f) The computer keeps crashing. It's that new software Maia installed.
____
____

g) That's Linda at the door. She's forgotten her keys.
____
____

5 Write some assumptions about people you know using *will*. For example, *Sam'll be having his coffee break at the moment.*

a) ____________________ at the moment.
b) ____________________ by now.
c) ____________________ by the time I'm 40.
d) ____________________ right now.
e) ____________________ ages ago.

6 Write sentences that are true for you using *will/won't* and *probably*.

a) I'll probably or I probably won't go out tonight.
b) ____________________ work this evening.
c) ____________________ go away at the weekend.
d) ____________________ become fluent in English.
e) ____________________ use the internet later.

8 Cyberspace (2)

Using discourse markers

You use discourse markers in both speech and writing to give your ideas a coherent structure and to help your listeners or readers follow what you want to say. For example, they are used to contrast ideas, to add information, to make concessions and to draw conclusions.

Contrasting two situations or ideas

Some of the words and phrases you can use are *but, nevertheless,* and *yet.*

But is the most common contrastive discourse marker in English. There are many common phrases using *but,* such as *but now* and *but more importantly.*

Nevertheless is similar to *but,* but it is more formal.
You use *yet* to show that something is surprising.

People used to think films were just crude entertainment, **but now** cinema is recognized as an art form.
That film was a box-office success, **but more importantly**, it set new artistic standards.
His argument contained some very logical points. It was, **nevertheless**, rather poorly constructed.
I don't eat very much, **yet** I'm a size sixteen.

Adding similar information

Some of the words and phrases you can use are *as well, as well as, also, not only (…but also)* and *what's more.*
Did you know that he can play the clarinet **as well**?
He thinks video games are an art form, **as well as** being a source of entertainment.
She's **also** been involved in creating some new computer graphics programs.
Not only do they offer the best visual quality on the market, their sound is probably the best you can get.
You should remember what you've learnt, and **what's more** you should be able to apply it in practical situations.

Note: When you use *Not only* in the initial position, as above, you invert the subject and the auxilliary. (See Unit 3 (2).)

Giving examples

When you want to exemplify a point you have just made, you can use *for example, for instance,* and *in particular.*
Video games have seen many changes in the last few years. **For example**/**For instance**, in the 1990s came the invention of full 3D images.

You can make changes in your office to make sure your working environment is the best for your health.
In particular, make sure that your desk is the right height and the monitor is at the right angle to your body.

Making concessions

This happens when someone makes a point or gives some facts, then concedes that there is contradictory information that seems to go against the argument. This part is introduced by words and phrases like *it's true, of course* and *certainly.*
He or she then dismisses this information and returns to the original direction of the arguement. This part is introduced by words and phrases like *however, but (then), still, even so, nevertheless* and *all the same.*

Video games do not necessarily encourage children to become violent in their own lives. Now, **it's true** that if a slightly disturbed child plays such games too much, then he might become more violent. **But then**, the majority of children are not disturbed, and there is no evidence that video games do those children any harm.

Drawing conclusions

Some of the words and phrases you can use to draw conclusions based on what you know are *so, so in this sense, this means that* and *after all.*
These games are played by people of all ages and all walks of life. **So in this sense** they are truly universal.
This means that we can expect to see a whole range of new games appearing on the market.
You shouldn't worry if your kids spend a lot of time playing video games – **after all**, it keeps them off the streets!

8 (2) Practice

1 Complete the following newspaper extracts with the discourse markers in the box.

~~after all~~ after all also as well as for instance nevertheless it's true that not only this means that yet

a) He believes that golf isn't as tough as tennis. 'Golf should be easy,' he said. ' After all , the ball never moves and you try to produce the same swing all the time.'

b) The assistant referee flagged for offside, but the referee waved play on and gave the goal ______

c) So, is the image of tango changing? 'Well, ______ years ago the men dominated,' says dancer Gustavo Russo, 'and technically they still lead in the dance, but these days it is more about the woman.'

d) There are nine different vaccines available in the UK to protect against meningitis, influenza, hepatitis, and typhoid, ______ all the usual childhood infections.

e) In exchange for investing in the company, control of at least part of the company may have to be transferred to the investor and ______ the original owners may lose overall control of the business.

f) The Government will offer all assistance to help British Aerospace to export its products. ______, it is orders that businesses need to provide jobs and to guarantee employment.

g) The rules for news coverage of court hearings in the UK differ drastically from many other countries. ______ are television cameras and recording equipment barred from court, but the media are ______ prohibited from photographing or even drawing a judge, juror or witness.

h) Beckham was nothing like match fit, ______ he was still picked in the starting eleven against Brazil.

i) How do we keep up with technology? ______, no sooner have you splashed out on all the latest all-singing all-dancing mobile than your friend is telling you that it is so 'last-year'.

2 Write the expressions in the box next to those in the sentences that have similar meaning.

but all things considered ~~but essentially~~ even so but in time but more specifically but now but then again

a) We always get to the quarter or semi-finals, **but basically** / but essentially we're just not good enough to get any further.

b) It's likely to be a software problem, **but on the other hand** / ______ it could always be something to do with the hard drive itself.

c) His work leaves a lot to be desired, **but more to the point** / ______ it's his I-don't-care attitude that I object to.

d) She's eighty-eight, **but nevertheless** / ______ she makes sure she walks at least a mile every day.

e) It might not seem it at this moment in time, **but eventually** / ______ you'll understand and everything will make sense.

f) Of course most businesses are concerned about their employees, **but at the end of the day** / ______, they're more concerned about the money.

g) Computers used to have a shelf-life of years, **but these days** / ______ they're outdated in a matter of months.

3 Put the discourse markers in *italics* into a natural position in these e-mail extracts.

a) Train is the best way to get here. ^But In case you decide to come by car, I'll ^also attach directions from the M6. *but; also*

b) I've forwarded this to David B, I think he may be away at the moment. *as well; but*

c) As for expenses, yes it's policy that you can claim for time spent at the meeting as well as travel. You could have spent that time working and getting paid for it, so it's only fair. Your claim must be in by the end of the month. *after all; but*

d) I guess we'll have to get Jane along to the meeting. This thing was her idea. And she'll be expecting to be included. *also; after all; what's more*

e) We could come the weekend after next. If you prefer, the weekend of 29th–30th is a possibility. *but; also*

9 *Law (1)*

Using modals to talk about the past

Here are some of the ways you can use modals to talk about the past.

To report speech or thought

The modals typically used for reporting speech and thought are *would ('d)* (to report *will*) and *could* (to report *can*).

'We'll take care of things for you,' they said

They said they**'d take** care of things for us.

'You can come with us – there's plenty of room in the car,' she told me.

She told me that I **could go** with them, as there was plenty of room in the car.

'This time next week I'll be lying on a tropical beach,' I thought.

I thought I**'d be lying** on a tropical beach this time next week.

'I'll have finished the work by the end of the day', he promised.

He promised that he **would have finished** the work by the end of the day.

To speculate or make deductions

The modals typically used for speculating and making deductions are *would ('d), could, might, must* and *can't*. When you use them to talk about the past, you use them with the perfect or perfect continuous infinitive.

I think they**'d have arrived** by now if they were coming at all.

All this damage **couldn't have been caused** by just one person, could it? (passive)

The thief **might have got in** through an upstairs window.

I think I **must have left** my umbrella on the train.

Your glasses **can't have** just **disappeared** into thin air – they must be here somewhere.

The car **would have been travelling** pretty fast at the time of the accident.

I'm sure I **couldn't have been doing** more than sixty.

It **must have been raining** – the pavements are wet.

Is this the best you could do – you **can't have been trying** very hard!

When you speculate or make deductions about the past, you can use *must* only in affirmative sentences, and *can* in negative sentences.

They **must have been** really worried to have called the police.

He **can't have known** about the meeting – it's not like him to be late.

To comment or criticize

The modals typically used for commenting and criticizing are *could, should, might* and *ought* to. When you use them to talk about the past, you use them with the perfect or perfect continuous infinitive.

You were lucky – you **could** easily **have been injured**. (passive)

You really **shouldn't have left** without apologizing, you know.

I know I **ought to have had** the car **serviced** sooner. (passive)

You **shouldn't have been watching** TV until two in the morning.

You use *could have* and *might have* with the stress on the main verb to express annoyance.

They **could have told** us they were going to be late – we were really worried.

You **might have informed** me! You knew how important this job was to me!

If you think that someone has been thoughtless, you can use `How could you?' on its own or with an infinitive.

How could you? You knew that was my favourite CD and you lost it!

How could you do such a thing?

How could you have been so stupid?

9 (1) Practice

1 Rewrite the second sentence using the most appropriate modal *must, can't* or *might* so the meaning is similar.

a) My e-mail wasn't working earlier. The server was probably down.
The server must've been down.

b) The wedding was amazing. I'm sure it cost them a fortune.
____

c) I don't know what time it was, but it was still light. So I'm sure it wasn't that late.
____

d) Where is he? Do you think it's possible he's got lost?
____________________?

e) Where is she? Perhaps she didn't get the message.
____

f) You didn't get my e-mail? Maybe I sent it to your old address.
____

g) You waited for two hours? I imagine that wasn't much fun.
____

h) £60 can't be right. Surely they've overcharged us.
____

2 Complete the newspaper stories with the modals in the box and the verb in brackets.

should should would

When 'A' is not enough

A student at a Memphis high school in Michigan is suing his school for $25 000 and is seeking to have the grade he was given for a work-experience project changed. Brian Delekta, an 11th grade student, worked at his mother's law office as part of his school's work-experience programme and on completion was awarded a grade 'A'. But the student believes this (a) __________ (be) an 'A+', which (b) __________ (further/increase) his chances of becoming the highest ranking student in the class, an important achievement in the US. Delekta also claims that the school (c) __________ (not/release) the class rankings before the case was settled.

must should would

Dangerous spectator sport

The Philadelphia baseball team is being sued by a spectator who was hit by a ball. The spectator tried to catch the ball, but instead it hit him in the head. He filed a lawsuit against the team alleging the ball (d) __________ (not/hit) him if the protective backstop at the Stadium had been wider and angled differently. Specifically, the claimant is seeking $50,000 for his eye injuries because the stadium (e) __________ (provide) more protection for spectators. The Phillies' defence lawyer claims that as a regular attendee at baseball games the claimant (f) __________ (be) fully aware of the dangers, especially as there are warnings on the back of every ticket, on posted signs and through regular public announcements.

must should would would

Who's the rat?

An episode of NBC's reality show, Fear Factor, in which the contestants were expected to drink blended dead rats, has resulted in the television network being sued for $2.5 million by a man who claims they (g) __________ (warn) viewers in advance about the content of the show. Austin Aitkin from Cleveland, Ohio, believes that watching the show caused him to become dizzy and light-headed. He began to feel sick and ran towards the bathroom. He claims (h) __________ (run) into the door frame as a result of his dizziness, injuring himself in the process. Aitkin says that he isn't concerned with winning money, but that the lawsuit (i) __________ (highlight) the harmful effects of TV for the public. Aitkin then told reporters that he (j) __________ (only/discuss) the complaint in more detail if he was paid for the interview.

3 Rewrite the sentences with a phrase using *could have* or *might have* to show you are annoyed.

a) Why didn't you tell me you'd be late?
You could've told me you'd be late!

b) Why didn't she wait for us?
____________________!

c) Why didn't you warn me about it?
____________________!

d) Why wasn't he a bit more helpful?
____________________!

9 Law (2)

Inversion after *neither/nor, so & such*

Neither/nor

When you use *neither* or *nor* to add a further negative comment to a negative sentence with the verb *be*, you invert the subject and verb. The subject after *neither/nor* is affirmative.

They weren't hungry and **nor were they** thirsty.

When you use an auxiliary or a modal auxiliary, you invert the subject and auxiliary.

Heinz doesn't contribute to class very much, **nor does he** put much effort into his homework.
Jon hasn't seen him lately, and **neither has he** talked to him on the phone.
He wasn't seeking recognition, and **nor did he** appreciate it when it came.
I was not at all impressed by the acting, and **neither could I** understand half of the dialogue.

A less formal alternative is to use *not…either*, in which case there is no inversion.
I wasn't at all impressed by the acting, and I **couldn't** understand half of the dialogue, **either**.

So/such

When you use *so* or *such* at the beginning of a sentence with the verb *be*, you invert the subject and verb. *So* is usually followed by an adjective, a form of *be*, and a subject.

So excited is she by the idea of winning the car, she has spent all her money on tickets.
So disgusted was he by the service, he decided to complain to the manager.
So intricate is the plot of the novel that even the author himself has said he finds it difficult to follow.

So can sometimes be followed by an adverb. Here you invert the subject and auxiliary.
So well did he dance, he was chosen to play one of the dancers in Billy Elliot.

Such is followed by *be* and a subject.
Such was the scale of the damage, it was hard to imagine how normality could ever be restored.
Such were his skills, even the most experienced lawyers feared him.
Such was the weather that even the most experienced windsurfers stayed at home.

Note: You tend to use these structures in formal contexts and they are more usually found in writing than in speech. In less formal contexts, you do not use inversion.

The plot of the novel is so intricate that even the author himself has said he finds it difficult to follow.
He danced so well that he was chosen to play one of the dancers in Billy Elliot.

So & *neither/nor* in short answers

In conversation, you can also invert the subject and auxiliary when you use *so, neither* or *nor* at the beginning of a short answer to show agreement. You use *so* to agree with an affirmative statement and *neither/nor* to agree with a negative statement.

I have done everything I can to help her. **So have I**.
I'm wondering what she's going to do next. **So am I**.
I don't know what all the fuss is about. **Nor do I**.
I didn't really follow the plot of the movie. **Nor did I**.
I wouldn't like to live in one of those new flats. **Neither would I**.

When the tense is present simple or past simple in the affirmative, there is no auxiliary in the main sentence, but when you are making a short answer you use the auxiliaries *do, does* or *did*.
I **hate** that first day back at work after the holidays. **So do I**!
I **thought** you weren't allowed to use a mobile phone when driving. **So did I**.

9 (2) Practice

1 Complete these newspaper extracts, beginning with *so* or *such*.

a) _________ was the hectic pace of the game, that it came as no surprise when Miller scored his second goal shortly before half-time.

b) _________ is the attraction and fascination of reality shows that talentless show-offs and casting agency rejects have become in-demand celebrities.

c) _________ outraged by her dismissal were Jones's co-workers that they organized a walkout and demanded her immediate reinstatement.

d) _________ has been the show's popularity that it is still running more than forty years after its opening night.

e) _________ nervous was he that he would forget his lines.

2 Write an alternative sentence beginning for these extracts, starting with the word underlined.

a) She is <u>so</u> technophobic / So technophobic is she that almost every e-mail she sends is accompanied by a phone call to confirm its receipt.

b) The weather was <u>such</u> / __________________ that the race had to be postponed.

c) He was <u>so</u> hungry / __________________ that he devoured almost the entire contents of the fridge.

d) The importance of training is <u>such</u> / __________________ that we have committed ourselves to a programme of investment of £1.7 billion.

e) The tackle was <u>so</u> ferocious / __________________ that Keane faces a minimum six match suspension.

3 Rewrite the extracts beginning with the word given so that the meaning is similar. You will need to change adjectives to nouns and vice versa.

a) So angry are they about increased ticket prices that many fans are staying away in protest.
Such is their anger about increased ticket prices that many fans are staying away in protest.

b) Schumacher was so dominant that for a few seasons the result of the F1 driver's championship was a foregone conclusion.
Such __________________ that for a few seasons the result of the F1 driver's championship was a foregone conclusion.

c) Such was his determination to get back a regular first team place that he trained well into the night.
So __________________ that he trained well into the night.

d) Such was their desperation that a single grain of rice was worth fighting over.
So __________________ that a single grain of rice was worth fighting over.

4 Rewrite the sentences linking the ideas with *neither* or *nor*.

a) The staff weren't friendly and they weren't helpful.
The staff weren't friendly and nor were they helpful.

b) The software is not as easy to install and it's not as user-friendly.
____
____

c) If he isn't going to say anything then I won't either.
____
____

5 Write responses agreeing to the statements using *So do I, Neither did I, So can I* etc.

a) I can speak English. __________
b) I can't speak Arabic. __________
c) I've never been to Spain. __________
d) I've been to the UK. __________
e) I don't like football. __________
f) I prefer white wine to red. __________
g) I didn't go out last night. __________
h) I live with my parents. __________
i) I'm not tired. __________
j) I'm going out tonight. __________
k) I enjoy studying. __________

6 Which of the statements in exercise 5 are true for you? (Circle) the responses to these statements.

10 *Firsts (1)*

Contrast

You can use several discourse markers to contrast two ideas.

But

You can use *but* to link two contrasting ideas within a sentence. It links two equal **main clauses**, and always comes at the beginning of the second clause. There is often a comma between the two clauses.

I studied German when I was at school, **but** I never liked it much.

I like playing golf **but** I hate watching it on TV.

But can also join two other elements, such as two adverbials or two adjectives.

I often go out **on a Saturday night**, but **never on a weekday**.

The weather was **warm** but **windy**.

You can also use *but* in informal language to introduce a contrasting idea at the beginning of a new sentence.

Golf's a fine pastime and is a great way of spending some time outdoors. **But** watching it on TV can be very tedious.

However

You can also use *however* to link contrasting ideas. It is more formal than *but*.

There are three possible positions.

- at the beginning of the sentence, followed by a comma
  I'm really bad at remembering names sometimes. **However**, I never forget a face.
- after the subject of the sentence or after an adverbial, usually with commas before and after it.
  I never used to come first in anything in school. My brother, **however**, seemed to be constantly winning prizes.
  He showed great promise in athletics in his teens. Later on, **however**, he gradually lost interest.
- at the end of the sentence, preceded by a comma
  He showed great promise in athletics in his schooldays. He never fulfilled this early promise, **however**.

You could use *but* instead of *however* only in the first of these three positions, and then it is not followed by a comma.

On the other hand

You use *on the other hand* to balance two ideas that contrast with each other but do not contradict each other. You can use it when you are trying to be fair and moderate.

Well, yes, hospitals are losing money. **On the other hand**, they are saving lives, and surely that's more important.

You can also use *on the one hand* to introduce the first of the two balancing ideas, and *on the other (hand)* to introduce the second idea.

On the one hand, I felt sorry for him and was ready to help him in any way I could. **On the other (hand)**, I thought he was partly to blame for what had happened to him.

Whereas, while

You can use *whereas* or *while* (or *whilst*) to balance two ideas that contrast with each other, but do not contradict each other. They link a **main clause** with a **subordinate clause**, and are used at the beginning of the subordinate clause. The subordinate clause can come either first or second in the sentence. You put a comma between the two clauses, but not after *whereas* or *while*.

Whereas most people prefer to work a nine to five day, I prefer to have a flexible timetable.

I prefer to have a flexible timetable, **whereas** most people prefer to work a nine to five day.

You can usually choose which idea you want to put into the main clause and which into the subordinate clause.

Most people prefer to work a nine to five day, **while** I prefer to have a more flexible timetable.

10 (1) Practice

1 Look at the graph and complete the descriptions with *but, however* or *whereas.*

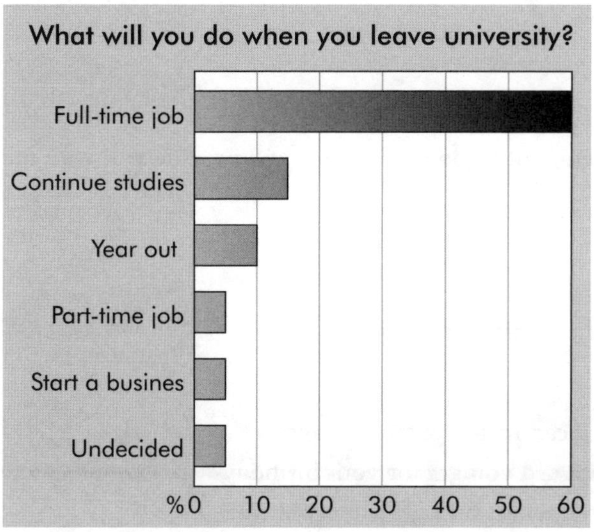

a) The majority of students have plans for when they leave university. ___________, 5% remain undecided.

b) 60% will look for employment in established companies, ___________ 5% intend start their own business.

c) 65% of undergraduates say they will look for employment. 5%, ___________, say they only want part-time work.

d) About a quarter of all graduates do not intend to look for work at all, ___________ will either continue studying or take a year out.

e) ___________ most of those going on to do further studies will specialize in the same subject as their first degree, about one in five intend to study a different subject.

2 Choose the correct alternative.

Contrary to popular belief, Thomas Edison didn't actually 'invent' the light bulb. He did, (a) *but/however/whereas,* improve upon a well-established 50-year-old idea. In the 1880s, the idea of electric lighting was not new, (b) *but/however/while* up to that time nothing had been developed that was remotely practical for home use. (c) *But/However/Whereas* existing electric lighting was cumbersome and lasted only a few minutes, Edison, in 1879, managed to produce something not only of convenient size, (d) *but/on the other hand/whereas* which burned for thirteen and a half hours. The success of his electric light brought Thomas Edison to new heights of fame and wealth as electricity spread around the world. His various electric companies continued to do well on their own, (e) *but/however/ whereas* in 1889 they were brought together to form Edison General Electric. Despite the use of Edison in the company title (f) *but/however/ whereas,* he never controlled this company and when it merged with its leading competitor in 1892, Edison was dropped from the name and the company became simply General Electric.

3 Complete these famous quotations with *however* or *whereas.*

a) From what we get, we can make a living; what we give, ___________, makes a life. (Arthur Ashe, tennis player and AIDS campaigner)

b) ___________ in art nothing worth doing can be done without genius, in science even a very moderate capacity can contribute to a supreme achievement. (Bertrand Russell, mathematician and philosopher)

c) You are never given a wish without also being given the power to make it come true. You may have to work for it, ___________ (Richard Bach, author)

d) Change is scientific, ___________ progress is a matter of controversy. (Bertrand Russell, mathematician and philosopher)

4 Combine the halves of these famous quotations.

a) I don't know the key to success, but… ☐
b) Nearly all men can stand adversity, but… ☐
c) Everyone is born with genius, but… ☐
d) Friends may come and go, but… ☐
e) He who asks is a fool for five minutes, but… ☐

1) most people only keep it a few minutes. (Edgard Varese, composer)
2) if you want to test a man's character, give him power. (Abraham Lincoln, US president)
3) he who does not ask remains a fool forever. (Chinese proverb)
4) the key to failure is trying to please everybody. (Bill Cosby, actor and comedian)
5) enemies accumulate. (Thomas Jones, author)

5 Tick (✓) the three quotes in exercises 3 and 4 that you like the best.

10 Firsts (2)

Patterns with *get*

You can use *get* in many different ways. Here are some of them, but a good dictionary will provide you with many more, and tell you the patterns in which they occur.

Become

When you use *get* with an adjective it means 'become'.

Things **got exciting** towards the end of the evening.

Are you **getting cold**?

Obtain/receive

When you use *get* with an object (noun phrase or pronoun), it can mean 'obtain' or 'receive'.

It would be a good idea to **get professional advice**.

I went back home to **get a coat and umbrella**.

I'd like you to **get some information for me**.

What did you **get** for your birthday?

Run upstairs and **get me my slippers**.

Succeed

Get + *to*-infinitive means 'succeed in doing something' or 'have the chance or opportunity to do something'.

I finally **got to meet** my hero in person.

Did you **get to talk** to your boss in the end?

Start

Get + *-ing* means 'start doing something'.

Let's **get going** then, or we'll be late.

There'll be lots of people to feed – we'd better **get cooking**.

Persuade/cause

Get + object + *to*-infinitive, or *get* + object + *-ing,* means 'ask or persuade someone to do something'.

I've been trying to **get him to sign** these papers.

I always **got the neighbours to look after** the house while I was away.

After a long time and a lot of effort, I finally **got them singing** in unison.

We promise we**'ll get your computer system running** perfectly by this time tomorrow.

You can also use *have* in this structure. (See Unit 12 (2).)

Make something *move*

Get + object + adverbial (prepositional phrase or adverb) means `make something move to a different place or position'.

I **couldn't get the top off the bottle**.

We **must get food into the area** as quickly as possible.

Get in passive structures

You can use *get* instead of *be* in passives. This use is more informal and is sometimes called the ***get* passive**.

My camera **got damaged** during the journey.

She **got promoted** last year.

In addition, you can use *get* instead of *have* in the structure '*get* something *done*'.

If you want to sell something, **get** it **valued** by a genuine dealer.

I **got** my wallet **stolen** when I was on holiday.

Phrasal verbs

Get combines with a particle to form a large number of phrasal verbs, for example:

What **are** you **getting at**? I don't understand. (= what are you trying to say)

You have to watch her – she'll cheat if she thinks she can **get away with** it. (= do it without being caught)

I've had flu and it's taken me a lot time to **get over** it. (= recover)

10 (2) Practice

1 Which word or words in each of these newspaper extracts can be replaced with a form of *get*? Cross it out and write the correct form of *get*.

a) The rescue team ~~received~~ got the call at about 7.40pm and took nearly two hours to reach Ms Woodroffe and a further hour to find Mr Bowden.

b) The Arsenal players surrounded the referee and somehow persuaded him to change his decision and award a free kick to them instead.

c) The forecast is that things will more than likely become a lot worse for the company before they start to see any turnaround in fortune.

d) In some health authorities you are lucky if you manage to see a specialist within two months of being diagnosed. Some patients I spoke to waited up to six months.

e) 'It seemed that drumming was the only thing I was any good at. I was fired from just about every other job I ever had,' Jones said.

f) The concert sold out in less than an hour and some of those who were lucky enough to buy tickets are now reselling them at up to 20 times their face value.

g) 'After the injury I became really quite depressed knowing I would probably miss out on the Olympics,' said Evans.

h) Shoppers can obtain generally obtain much better deals by buying products abroad via the internet.

i) The manager said he would have his head shaved if Burton progressed to the next round of the tournament.

2 Complete the sentences with *get* and the words in *italics*.

a) The boxes are quite heavy. I'll get someone to help you with them. *someone / help*

b) The gig was great and we ______________ afterwards. *meet / the band*

c) You didn't see me? I think you need ______________! *your eyes / test*

d) We really should ______________ if we want to catch the 6.30 bus. *go*

e) Do you need a lift to the station or have you already ______________ you? *someone / take*

f) Did you ______________ that mp3 player or did you find out whose it was? *keep*

g) You should ______________ your computer. If he can't ______________, then no-one can. *Alex / look at; get it / work*

h) Unfortunately, I didn't ______________ to Jim before he left. *speak*

i) You need your own key? Okay, I'll ______________ for you this afternoon. *one / cut*

j) I hear you ______________ at the weekend. Was anything stolen? *break into*

k) Fred's not here at the moment, but I'll ______________ later. *him / call you back*

3 Complete the sentences using the words in the box and the structure *get something done.*

it / check over	it / cut	~~it / look at~~
photos / print	some photocopying / do	

a) There's something wrong with my camera. I need to get it looked at.

b) I need to make a copy of this article. Do you know where I can ______________?

c) Your computer keeps crashing? You ought to ______________

d) My memory card's full. Do you know a good place ______________?

e) I like your hair! Where do you ______________?

4 Complete the sentences so they are true for you. For example, *I hope one day I'll get the chance to go to Australia. I really need to get going with my exam revision.*

a) I hope one day I'll get the chance to ______________

b) I really need to get going with ______________

c) It's sometimes hard to get my friends to ______________

d) I'm not sure I'll ever get to ______________

e) I need to get my ______________

11 Stories (1)

Telling stories

Staging

Stories are often told in five stages.

1. Introduction: This signals that the story is about to begin and draws attention from the listener.

Have I ever told you about the time I got stranded in Ramsgate?

This is one of my father's stories from the Second World War.

2. Background: This helps the listener to identify the time, place, people, activity and situation of the story.

It was the first time I'd been there and I didn't know my way around.

It was just after the war and things were still a bit chaotic.

3. Problem or complicating action: This is the core narrative component providing the answer to the question 'What happened?', or 'What was the problem?'

I felt in my pockets but all my money had gone.

Suddenly the boat tilted dramatically.

4. Resolution: This tells the listener how it all ended; how the problems were resolved.

Finally I managed to borrow some money from a passing stranger.

In the end the storm died down and they were able to venture outside.

5. Comment: This makes the point of the story clear, and signals that the story has ended.

I felt such an idiot.

But it turned out to be one of the best things that ever happened to him.

Features

These are some common features of oral story-telling. Some of the examples come from well-known fairy tales.

Reporting thoughts directly

She looked at the wolf and thought, `That doesn't look like my grandmother!'

Reporting speech directly

The witch stood facing the mirror and said `Mirror, mirror, on the wall, who's the fairest of them all?'

Repetition

And Pinocchio's nose started to grow, and the more he lied, the more it grew, and the more it grew, the more he lied.

Asides to the listener

And she sat there all day, every day, staring into the fire. Who would have thought that a child could be so sad?

Adding detail

It was just like a cottage from a storybook, with a thatched roof and a garden full of flowers.

Making the story personal

Anyway, she decided to try to walk to the nearest village, and I suppose I'd probably have done the same.

Using the voice

Storytellers use their voices to add dramatic effect in a number of ways, including the following.

Using stress for dramatic effect

And I'll HUFF and I'll PUFF and I'll BLOW your house down.

Pausing for dramatic effect

I opened the door and guess what...there was nobody there.

11 (1) Practice

1 Put the story extracts a–f into the correct order.

a) Shrek is not at all happy about this and sets off to find Lord Farquaad and convince him to take the fairytale creatures back where they belong so he can once again live in peace in his swamp. Lord Farquaad accepts, but under one condition. Shrek must first go and find the beautiful young princess Fiona, who will become Farquaad's bride. Accompanied by his faithful friend, Donkey, Shrek sets off on his quest. He manages to find and rescue the princess from a fire-breathing dragon and deliver her to Lord Farquaad. ☐

b) During the wedding ceremony in which Lord Farquaad and Princess Fiona were supposed to be married, Shrek rescues her one more time and evil Lord Farquaad is eaten by the dragon. ☐

c) This story takes place once upon a time in a faraway land called Duloc. Happily living alone in a swamp in a forest in Duloc is an ogre called Shrek. ☐

d) In the meantime though, princess Fiona, who is actually an ogre herself and only takes human form during daylight hours, has fallen in love with Shrek and does not want to marry Lord Farquaad. ☐

e) But that wasn't at all the end of the story. ☐

f) One day, the heartless ruler of Duloc, the midget Lord Farquaad, banishes all the fairytale creatures from the land and sends them to live in Shrek's swamp. ☐

g) Shrek and Fiona get married themselves and live happily ever after with Donkey in Shrek's swamp. ☐

2 Match the extracts a–g in exercise 1 with the story sections 1–4.

1) introduction/background ☐
2) problem ☐ ☐ ☐
3) resolution ☐ ☐
4) final comment ☐

3 Match the extracts with story features a–f.

1) reporting thoughts directly ☐
2) reporting speech directly ☐
3) repetition ☐
4) asides to the listener ☐
5) adding detail ☐
6) making the story personal ☐

a) He thumped and he thumped and he thumped.
b) 'I want you to meet me downtown at seven o'clock . We will have dinner together,' Von Gerhard said.
c) As Henry trudged upstairs, banished to his bedroom, his brother was grinning at him. 'I'll get you next time,' Henry thought to himself.
d) It was the most disgusting sight. I'd never seen anything like it, and hope I never will again.
e) The wood was dense and overgrown, dark and frightening.
f) He was listening to a CD Walkman, you know, the ones that were popular a few years back.

4 Identify and underline examples of the story features in exercise 3 in this story.

Late one Saturday night, a Dr Eckersall was driving home. It was a windy and rainy night, you know, the sort of night when you just want to get home as quickly as possible. As he slowed up for an intersection he saw a young girl beckoning him for a lift. 'What on earth is a youngster like you doing out here all alone at this time of night?' he asked. 'It's too long a story to tell you now,' said the girl. 'Please, please take me home. I'll explain everything there.' The doctor set off and drove to the address she had given him. As he pulled up before the shuttered house, he turned around to speak to the girl. But she was gone. 'What the devil?' thought the doctor. He knocked on the door of the house, and again and then again. At long last the door opened. A grey-haired and very tired-looking man opened the door and peered out at him. 'A young girl gave me this address a while back. I drove her here and …' began the doctor. 'Yes, yes, I know,' interrupted the man wearily. 'This happens on this day every year. That young girl, sir, was my daughter. She was killed in an automobile accident at that intersection where you saw her ten years ago…'

11 *Stories (2)*

The future seen from the past

You can use the following structures to talk about something that was expected to happen in the past, but didn't.

Was/were going to + infinitive

I **was going to phone** you, but I forgot.
We **were going to go** to the cinema last night, but we couldn't be bothered.
At first I **wasn't going to apply** for the job, but I'm glad I did in the end.

Was/were supposed to + infinitive

I **was supposed to be working** yesterday, but I managed to get the day off.
Her new book **was supposed to be published** last October, but there were some problems. (passive)
They **were supposed to have gone** away on holiday last week, but James got the flu.

Was/were due to + infinitive

They **were due to arrive** at twelve, but they got held up.
The old factory **was due to be demolished** last week. (passive)
I **was due to start** writing my new paper today, but I didn't get round to it.

Note: You can also use these structures if the expected or planned event is in the future, but will not happen.

I **was going to phone** you tonight, but if you've got time for a chat now, I won't need to.
I **was supposed to be working** tomorrow, but I've managed to get the day off.
The old factory **was due to be demolished** next week, but plans for it have changed. (passive)

Was/were on the verge of + -ing

The structure *on the verge of* suggests that the event was imminent. You can use *just* for emphasis.
I **was on the verge of leaving** the house when the phone rang.
They **were just on the verge of cracking** the code, but the other team got there first.

Was/were about to + infinitive

This structure also suggests that the event was imminent. Again you can use *just* for emphasis.
We **were about to cross** the border into Jordan when I realized that I had forgotten my passport.
I **was just about to go and collect** the kids from school when you phoned me.

Be to + infinitive

You can use *be to* + infinitive to explain that a formal arrangement had been made, whether or not the arrangement was actually carried out. This is common in news reports and other formal situations.

The president **was to visit** the town the following week, and already the streets were full of flags.
The new school hall **was to be opened** by the local MP, but he cancelled at the last minute. (passive)
We **were to have met** the artist at a reception, but she didn't turn up.

Would

You can often use the modal *would* to talk about the future in the past, especially after verbs such as *imagine, expect* and *think.*

I **had** always **imagined you would become** a musician.
We **had expected** that they **would bring** some warm clothes, considering the climate.
We **hadn't thought** it **would take** us so long to get there.

11 (2) Practice

1 Complete these extracts using *was/were going to* and the verbs in the box.

escape leave say ~~stay~~ not tell walk by

a) We were going to stay the night, but thought we'd better make a break for it before the weather worsened even more.

b) 'I love you like…' – he ________ 'like a sister', but he suddenly changed his mind. 'I love you to distraction, Rosie,' he said instead.

c) Just the other month, I met my mother in Kensington High Street. I ________, but she grasped my sleeve. 'Why are you ignoring me?' she asked.

d) 'It was absolutely necessary!' Frank snapped. 'They ________ and my orders were quite explicit: I was to stop them at all cost.'

e) 'Why ________ you ________ without saying goodbye?' he asked, as Marilyn, head bowed, closed the door in front of her and put her bags down.

f) I ________ her, hoping she'd see things differently having slept on it, but she refused to go to bed until I had explained all.

2 Rewrite the extracts so the meaning is similar, using the words in *italics*.

a) 'I thought the plan was for this to be a working dinner,' I said as Stella offered to fill my glass yet again. 'Oh, it's work, all right,' she replied with a smile. 'Believe me.' *supposed*
'I thought this was supposed to be a working dinner,' I said as Stella offered…

b) The plan was for me to leave at five-thirty in the afternoon. At five o'clock I was dressed and ready. Then the phone rang with the news. *due*
I ________. At five o'clock…

c) She looked as though she was just about to say something, but she turned and walked out of the room in silence. *verge*
She looked as though ________, but she turned…

d) I should have been in a meeting first thing, but the night before was taking its toll and I just couldn't face it. *supposed*
I ________, but the night before…

e) He had almost fallen asleep when he heard footsteps on the landing. *verge*
He ________ when he heard…

f) We had planned to get a taxi, but decided stroll home along the river instead. *going*
We ________, but decided to…

g) We had expected him to arrive on Monday, not Tuesday. *would*
We had expected that ________, not Tuesday.

3 Rewrite the extracts so the meaning is similar using *was/were to*.

a) They said play would resume at one-thirty, but at a quarter past the heavens opened yet again.
Play ________,
but at a quarter past…

b) We had planned to meet for dinner, but the paparazzi seemed to know our every move and the venue was changed five times.
We ________,
but the paparazzi…

c) The doctors originally planned to discharge the president on Tuesday, but decided to keep him in for a further night. The president ________,
but doctors decided…

4 Complete the sentences about things in your life that you expected to happen but didn't. For example, *I was going to go out last night, but I was just too tired.*

a) I was going to ________, but ________

b) I was supposed to ________, but ________

c) I was on the verge of ________, but ________

12 Words (1)

-ever

The suffix *-ever* can be combined with question words to create *whoever, whatever, whichever, whenever, wherever,* and *however.* These words are used to mean

- it doesn't matter who, what, which, when, where or how
- any person who, any thing that, any time that, any place that, any way/method that

Whoever, whatever and *whichever*

- These words act as either the **subject** or **object** of the clause they introduce.

If death occurs at home, **whoever** discovers the body should contact the family doctor. (subject)
Whoever you marry, make sure he can cook and clean. (object)

Whatever is going to happen, there's no point in worrying too much beforehand. (subject)
Whatever you say, it won't make any difference. (object)

Whichever suits you best would be the one to choose. (subject)
Whichever you choose, I'm sure you'll be satisfied. (object)

- *Whatever* and *whichever* are sometimes determiners, coming before a noun.

Whatever brand you use, be careful to test it on a small area before trying to remove the stain. (object)
Whichever school seems best for your child – that's the one to choose. (subject)

- *Whatever* and *whichever* + noun can also be part of a prepositional phrase.

If you can't keep the appointment **for whatever reason**, please inform us three days in advance.
You can apply **in whichever language** you like: English, Arabic or Punjabi.

- *Whatever* (or *whatsoever*) can also be an adverb after a noun phrase with negative meaning. In this case it is very emphatic.

There is **no scientific evidence whatever** to support these theories.

Whenever, wherever and *however*

These words act as the **adverbial** of the clause they introduce.
He just does exactly what he wants, **whenever** he wants.
Whenever I go to Bournemouth I always visit my mother.

Note that as in the last example, *whenever* can also indicate repetition, in the sense of 'every time that'.

Sit **wherever** you can – there may not be enough chairs.
Wherever I went, I found that people were very friendly.

However you do it, just make sure it's done by this time tomorrow.
You can't just spell words **however** you like.

However can also come before an adjective or an adverb.
You should always tell the truth, **however difficult** it may be. (adjective)
However fast you drive, it will be impossible to get there on time. (adverb)

Open-ended lists

You can also use all the words formed with *-ever* to finish an open-ended list.
Borrow the money from your mum, dad, brother, **whoever**.
I don't really mind what we do. Go to the cinema, go out for a meal, stay in and watch a video, **whatever**.
Come round any time, tomorrow morning, this evening, **whenever**.

12 (1) Practice

1 Complete the sentences with an appropriate word formed with *-ever*.

a) Can you pass this on to the new guy, John, Jim, or _whatever_ his name is?

b) You can use the computer ____________ you like. You don't need to ask.

c) You can drop me anywhere near the station – ____________ you like.

d) ____________ wins will play either Brazil or Italy in the next round.

e) You can borrow ____________ many CDs you like.

f) ...so they are the rules. And ____________ has the most points at the end of the game is the winner.

g) It's meant to be a surprise party, so don't tell Sam ____________ you do.

h) You choose – I'll have ____________ one you don't want.

i) Coffee or tea is fine – ____________ is easiest.

j) My computer keeps crashing ____________ I run that new photo software.

k) You can invite ____________ you like as long as you don't invite Harry.

2 Complete the sentence with an appropriate word formed with *-ever*.

a) Wear anything you like – jeans, skirt, t-shirt, _whatever._

b) Call round anytime – five, six, __________

c) I don't mind how they're done – poached, scrambled, boiled, __________

d) You can invite anyone you like – colleagues, neighbours, people from the pub, __________

e) I don't mind what we eat – Chinese, Indian, Thai, __________

f) We can go anywhere you like – the Louvre, Notre Dame, the Eiffel Tower, __________

3 Write similar sentences to those in exercise 2. For example, *We can listen to music, watch a DVD, play a computer game, whatever.*

a) ______________________________
______________________________, whatever.

b) ______________________________
______________________________, whoever.

c) ______________________________
______________________________, whenever.

4 Rewrite the sentences so that the meaning is similar beginning with an appropriate word formed with *-ever*.

a) Whether we go by car or bus, we're bound to get stuck in traffic.
However we go, we're bound to get stuck in traffic.

b) It doesn't matter how long it takes, I can't stop until it's finished.
____

c) Every time I see him he seems to be texting someone.
____

d) They seem to be playing that same song in every bar we go in.
____

e) It doesn't matter who we play, we'll beat them.
____

f) It didn't matter what the weather was like, we'd always have to go for a long walk.
____

5 Complete the newspaper article with *whatever, whenever, wherever, whoever* or *however*.

Here's the news: I'm stressed out.

I'm getting stressed out about the words people stress. I find myself shouting at the radio (a) _________ they mispronounce things. People can speak (b) _________ they like in private, but when addressing the nation that's another matter. I used to be a TV reporter and newsreader myself, but it was different back then. (c) _________ was reading the news read the scripts and decided which words should be stressed in order to help make the message clearer. Personally, I would underline words on the autocue (d) _________ possible.

Today, all sorts of words are being erroneously stressed – prepositions, conjunctions, pronouns and parts of speech I don't even know the names of. What I do know, however, is that (e) _________ it is behind this trend, it's spreading like a virus and I now hear examples (f) _________ I go.

12 Words (2)

Patterns with *have*

You can use *have* to talk about results, arrangements, services, or unpleasant things that happened to someone.

Results

You can use *have* + *someone/something* + *-ing* (present participle) to say:

- that you successfully encouraged or persuaded someone to do something.
  The band soon **had the audience joining in**.
  In the end I **had them all dancing and singing**.
- that you managed to get a machine or animal to do something.
  When do you think you**'ll have the printer working** again?
  I **had the computer up and running** five hours after I'd started work on it.
  The deer were very tame, and she soon **had them eating** out of her hand.
- that something happened as the consequence of an action.
  Frank's over-enthusiastic guitar-playing **had all the neighbours complaining**.
  The party was a bit noisy; we **had the police knocking** on the front door at one point.

Arrangements

You can use the pattern *have* + *someone* + infinitive to say that someone did or will do something for you because you asked them to.

I **had a lawyer look into** the ownership of the building.
I **had my neighbours look after** the dog last weekend.
She**'s having someone come round** to give her a quote for the decorating work.
I**'ll have a friend of mine translate** that letter for you.

Services

You can use the pattern *have* + object + past participle to say that someone did or will do something for you. This structure is sometimes known as **causative *have***.

You use this structure for three main reasons.

To talk about things that someone does for you in order to improve your physical condition or appearance.

He**'s had his hair coloured** – you really notice the difference.
I**'m having my eyebrows tinted and shaped**.
Would you ever think about **having your lip pierced**?
My tooth was badly infected – I had to **have it extracted** in the end.
You can't read that – you ought to **have your eyes tested**.

To talk about repairs, services, and building operations that someone does to your house, car etc.

In Britain, a lot of people still **have their milk delivered** every day.
I**'m going to have my car serviced** before it breaks down completely.
We**'re having some of the roof tiles replaced** to stop the leak.
I'll have to **have my house valued** before I put it on the market.

Unpleasant things that happened to someone

I **had my bag stolen** by two young girls.
Have you ever **had your house broken into**?
He was caught speeding, and **had his driving licence taken away** for six months.
Note: *Get* can be used instead of *have*, especially in informal speech and when talking about negative events.

12 (2) Practice

1 Put the verb in brackets in these conversation extracts into the correct form: present participle, past participle or infinitive.

a) I turned round and he'd disappeared, just run off somewhere. He had me ______________ (panic) like mad, I'll tell you.

b) The new boss is a bit of a slave driver – he'll have you ______________ (do) everything if you're not careful.

c) I'm having Roberto ______________ (teach) me some Italian at the moment.

d) Pete's gone to the police – he's had his bike ______________ (steal)

e) I'm going to have somebody ______________ (look) at my car. It's making an awful noise.

f) Those road works are becoming a right pain. They've had loads of people ______________ (complain) about it.

g) You know my exam results weren't that great? Well, I've had my mother on the phone ______________ (go on) about them just about every night this week.

h) We had someone ______________ (come) and value the flat the other day. €200,000 would you believe.

i) They're going to have someone ______________ (meet) me at the airport, so I should be at the hotel before midnight.

2 Complete the newspaper extracts with a phrase using *have* and the words in *italics*.

a) Evans claims that for six weeks his ex-wife ____________________ him 24 hours a day.
a private detective/follow

b) The offer of free tickets last month ____________________ to the website that it crashed. *so many people/log on*

c) Have you seen Sam? He's ____________________ bright red. *his hair/dye*

d) The film tells the story of German entrepreneur Oscar Schindler who helped save the lives of thousands of prisoners by ____________________ in his factory. *them/work*

e) The gig ended with a medley of his most famous hits, which ______________ for more.
the crowd/scream

f) We do our shopping on the internet these days and ____________________ *it/deliver*

g) Her personal assistant ____________________ outside for almost an hour while she prepared herself for the interview. And she then ____________________ a document saying that only photographs of the interview passed by the actress herself could be used.
me/wait us/sign

3 Match the expressions with the pictures.

a) It had her tearing her hair out. ☐
b) It had them jumping for joy. ☐
c) It had everyone biting their nails. ☐
d) It had her cringing with embarrassment. ☐
e) He had us crying with laughter. ☐
f) He had the crowd eating out of his hand. ☐

1) 

2) 

3) 

4) 

5) 

6) 

13 *Conscience*

Special uses of the past simple

You have previously seen how the past simple is used to talk about unreal situations. (See for example unit 5 (1).)

If we **had** more money, we could improve the facilities for young people in the area.

If only the government **spent** more money on local transport.

I wish there **was** more interest in helping the homeless in this city.

Here are some other ways of talking about unreal, desired situations using the past simple.

It's (about/high) time

You use these phrases to point out that something must be done as soon as possible, possibly because it should have been done before. You can add emphasis by using *about* or *high*. You can sometimes use this structure to sound critical or annoyed.

It's time you **had** a holiday.

It's time he **started** earning his own living.

It's time we **went**.

It's time we **decorated** the kitchen.

I think **it's about time** they **told** us what's going on.

It's high time the politicians **stopped** talking and **started** doing something.

It's high time you **stopped** complaining.

You can use the past continuous, as well as the past simple, with this structure.

It's high time we **were leaving**, or we'll miss the last bus.

If you are asking a question using these phrases, you often begin your sentence with 'Don't you think…?'or 'Wouldn't you say…?'

Don't you think it's about time you **turned off** the TV and **started** doing your homework?

Would ('d) rather + subject + past simple

You use this structure to say that you have a strong preference that a situation should be changed. You can add emphasis by using *much* and *really*. You can use negative verb forms with this structure.

I'd rather you **came** with me.

Would you **rather** we **sat** by the window?

I'd rather you **didn't smoke** while I'm eating.

I'd rather we **left** a bit earlier tomorrow.

I'd much rather you **came** with me.

I'd really rather we **didn't set off** quite so early tomorrow.

You can also use the past continuous with this structure.

I'd rather all those people **weren't sitting** there and **listening**.

It's possible to use a present tense with this structure, but it sounds rather formal and does not occur very often.

I'd rather people **do** something concrete to help instead of just paying out money to ease their consciences.

If *would rather* is not followed by a subject, you use an infinitive, not the past simple.

I'd rather go with you.

I'd rather not set off quite so early tomorrow.

Would you rather sit by the window?

Attitudes

You can sometimes use the past simple or the past continuous to refer more tentatively (and therefore more politely) to a present state of mind.

I **wondered** whether you **were** free on Saturday – perhaps we could meet for a drink.

I **was wondering** whether you **were** free on Saturday.

13 Practice

1 Rewrite the sentences so the meaning is similar beginning with *I'd/We'd rather…* etc.

a) I'd prefer you to come on Friday.

____

b) We'd prefer the lessons to start at 9.30.

____

c) Please don't put any music on.

____

d) It would be better for him if you could e-mail him.

____

e) I'd prefer her to speak to me first.

____

2 Rewrite the sentences so that the meaning is similar beginning with *It's time…*

a) We really must be going.

____

b) You ought to start getting ready to go out.

____

c) I really should start cooking dinner.

____

d) You need to stop working now.

____

3 Rewrite the sentences so the meaning is similar beginning with the words given.

a) I'd like to be able to speak French.
I wish __________________________

b) Not working would be great.
If only __________________________

c) I can't go out this evening because I have so much to do.
If I ____________________________

d) It's raining, which means I can't go out.
I wish ________________________. Then
____

4 Complete the newspaper extracts using the words in *italics*.

a) The feeling is that bearing in mind his promises about unemployment from his election manifesto two years ago, it is about time the president started to do something about it. *about time / the president / start*

b) The presence of additives in cigarettes has contributed to the lowering of tar levels but obviously the government ____________________________ altogether. *would much rather / people / give up*

c) The protesters message is that ____________________________ talking about the environment and actually did something about it. *high time / politicians / stop*

d) '____________________________ to doing something and tackled this very important corporate crime issue that's actually going on at the moment,' Rossi said. *about time / our government / actually / get round*

e) 'I frequently ____________________________ turn back time and make a different decision, but that politics and that's life,' Campbell said. *wish / I / can*

f) In his resignation speech, Mr Simpson said he ____________________________ decisions for the good of the country not the good of the party. *would rather / the government / make*

g) Given that so many kinds of pollution are avoidable, ____________________________ something to bring an end to this needless damage. *really / high time / we all / do*

h) ____________________________ to overseas causes, much of the world's poverty would very soon be history. *If only / one per cent of the West's taxes / go*

5 Complete the sentences so they are true for you. For example, *It's high time that more money was spent on education. I'd much rather I had a job I liked for less money than a well-paid job that I hated.*

a) It's high time
____
____

b) It's about time
____
____

c) I'd much rather I
____
____

d) I wish
____
____

Notes